celebrations with
Polymer Clay

Sarajane Helm

Published by

kp **krause publications**
An F&W Publications Company

700 East State Street • Iola, WI 54990-0001
715-445-2214 • 888-457-2873
www.krause.com

Please call or write for our free catalog of publications. Our toll-free number to place an order or obtain a free catalog is 800-258-0929 or please use our regular business telephone, 715-445-2214.

Library of Congress Catalog Number: 2002113134

ISBN: 0-87349-521-7

Printed in the United States of America

Photos by Bob Grieser Photography unless otherwise indicated.

The following company or product names appear in the book:
Adobe® Photoshop®, Aleene's®, American Science and Surplus, Art Accent Beedz, Atlas® Pasta Machine, Brilliance Inks, Berol® Prismacolor®, Broderbund's® Print Shop®, Cernit™, Darling Designer Discs™, Fabrico Ink Pad, Fimo®, Fimo Bronzepulver, Fimo® Mix Quick™, Flecto® Varathane® Diamond™ Wood Finish (Interior), Formica™, JASI Slicer, Kato® Nu-Blade, Kemper, Masonite™, Melamine™, PearlEx™, Polyform™, Premo!® Sculpey™, Premo® Sculpey ™ Shapelets, Rustoleum®, Sanford® Prismacolor®, Saran™ With Cling®, SculpeyIII™, Sculpey™ Super Elasticlay®, Sculpey™ Super Flex®, Sculpey™ Super Slicer®, Shadex Scratch Art, Silly Putty, Sobo, Super Glue, Toastmaster® Platinum, Tulip®, Uptown™ Design Company, X-Acto™.

Sarajane Helm. Moons and stars cover the back of this child-size guitar. It's a mosaic work in progress. Complex work takes time.

Sarajane Helm. "Sun Canes" shown with the drawing used as a guide to building the canes.

DEDICATION

This book is dedicated with love to my family, friends, and fellow artisans with whom it is a delight and a privilege to celebrate our existence.

Many special thanks go to all the wonderfully creative people whose work is shared on the pages of this book.

CONTENTS

THE PROJECTS

Spring 53

Summer 79

Autumn 99

Winter 117

Janis Holler. "Dream, Time, Love" hand pin.

TIME

*"What is this life if, full of care,
We have no time to stand and
stare?"*

−Leisure, William Henry Davies

OUR AWARENESS OF THE PASSAGE OF TIME

is one of our common links as human beings. We note the seasons as they change, we observe the cycle of changes in ourselves as well, and in those around us. No matter what the belief behind it or the form of the ceremony, all human cultures have marked this understanding of the difference between Now and Then in one way or another – many share images and symbols, though the meanings of those can vary dramatically. Humans around the world and through the ages decorate our dwellings, belongings, and ourselves and create artwork ranging from the most humble to the grand, using elements of design that can be found in societies halfway across the world as well. The dot, the spiral, the wheel, the cross, the circle are all symbols of the continuity of time, following itself in a constant dance throughout the changing circuit of Night and Day, and then on to Spring, Summer, Autumn, and Winter.

Opposite: "Clay, Night and Day" cane collage by Sarajane Helm. Making a collage of your millifiore canes serves the same purpose as old-fashioned samplers – it's a record of what you have accomplished.

Right: Sarajane Helm. "Time Mask" polymer clay, watch parts, beads, yarns, and charms.

"Pocket Watch" back, watch parts and verdigris embossing powder.

Sarajane Helm. "Pocket Watch" front, stamped with Time to Fly #124086 from Uptown Design Co., and Antique Gold PearlEx powder.

decorative arts and design is seen side by side with stylistic influences from Egypt, Ireland, and New Zealand. This can be seen in fashion, jewelry, and interior decor. We are availing ourselves of the styles and forms from the earliest times of human history and also the most recent, with revivals of fashions from many eras of the 19th and 20th centuries seen in today's stores – as are reproductions of Greek statuary, Native American pottery and weaving, and Egyptian friezes. We have more historical information available to us in the form of ancient items and research than at any other time in human history. People of all backgrounds and cultures can visit museums, libraries, and use the Internet to see items from all over our world and its myriad cultural groups throughout the span of recorded history. It is interesting to note that much of the information we have about ancient times comes to us through its remaining art!

We mark the beginning of cycles, we mark the ends, and we mark the middles too! As individuals we are aware of the different flavors and smells, the sights and sounds of each time of year, even though many of us no longer live immersed as intimately within a natural setting as did our ancestors. As members of societies, religions, cultures, and other groups, we find shared experiences, common appreciation and understanding, and work toward common goals. We learn and grow in positive ways when those things are expressed creatively. Through mutual understanding, we have the power to take comfort in our troubles and to share in the bounty of joyous times. We have the ability to learn from all the ups and downs that occur in nature and in human lives. Through ritual and ceremony, by way of music, dance, and visual arts of all kinds, we can extend something of our beliefs and emotions across all the borders of age, place, language, and doctrine.

In this way, we form a line of continuity in the midst of our changes. We honor the existence of those in the past by our interest in ancient objects. The popular use of cultural images from Asia and Africa in

In our "modern" time, it is increasingly common for us to live apart from the land and its rhythms. Families now live much farther apart from their members than in the days when travel was arduous and slow. And yet, even though we disperse from our original groups, we take something of our cultures and training with us wherever we go. We look to find our identities and to bring a sense of belonging to the new ways, the new places, the new groups, as well as to rediscover a sense of connectedness with what has gone before. Through our own awareness and personal experiences, we join together and build new memories for days to come even as we mark our connection to those of the past, and of the journey we all take throughout time.

Kathleen Bolan. "Night and Day."

Photo by Jerry Anthony.

Because we take the time to commemorate events – births, education and graduations, weddings, deaths – we honor those involved, and intertwine that involvement to include ourselves. When we celebrate our reality, we make it more memorable and share in a tie that binds us all together; we can knowingly choose to do this in a positive way. We proclaim the existence of the fabric of life and acknowledge our place in the pattern within it.

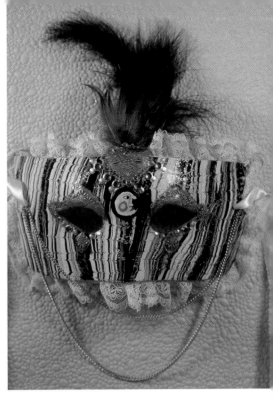

Sarajane Helm. These earrings were made using the cutout pieces from the eyeholes of "Moon Mask." Add a pendant with bells and you are ready to dance in the moonlight.

Sarajane Helm. "Moon Mask."

By creative efforts, we can make those memories and mementos more personal, and therefore more powerful. At Christmastime in our house, when dressing the tree with ornaments that were made in the first years of our marriage and that our children made over the last 20 years, we see strong visual evidence of a continuing line. The work of tiny hands now grown large is a statement of love and family that cannot be bought in stores. A paper ornament made by my grandmother has become a little crumpled over the decades, but I would not trade it for one of gold! When I place it on our tree, I remember it from when I was just a little girl and my Granny would share the delights of making things with me. I was blessed to have three grandparents and a mother who all strongly valued creativity and good workmanship. They passed these joys to me, and I have in my turn passed them to the next generation. The ornaments my children made are far more beautiful to me than any I could purchase, and they bring to mind those times (so quickly passed!). And because they are made with polymer clay, those items will be around to decorate our holidays for quite a while.

Z. Kripke. "Petroglyph" canes.

There are so many special occasions throughout the course of a year, and an endless variety of special ways to commemorate and celebrate them all. Each day is remarkable for one reason or another. There is no way for a single book to include them all, and I've only made a start at covering some favorites. The projects and techniques in this book can be adapted and made to fit many purposes and styles. Use your tools and creativity to make a personal statement in your daily living, and you will find a greater sense of being connected to your own life. Then take the next step and share the experience with those you love! Celebrate your existence now, and every day.

No matter what holidays or events you mark, no matter the style, make memories last by sharing the experience with those you love. Family is not only made by bloodlines; it is made by intent and by shared experience. Make yours beautiful! If you have not done so already, please start today.

Sarajane Helm

Set 1 from the Internet Miniature Masks Swap 2002. From the top left these were made by: Judith Skinner, Bill Girard, Ronnie, Colleen "Sunni" Bergeron, Gail Teunis, Sarajane Helm, Sarajane Helm, Rose Mary Martin, Sarajane Helm, Lisa Carlson, Sarajane Helm, Rose Mary Martin.

Set 2 from the Internet Miniature Masks Swap 2002. From the top left these were made by: Melody Steeples, Denise Standifer, Janet Hoy, Sarajane Helm, Denise Standifer, Judith Skinner, Denise Standifer, Dawn Dykes, Tonja Lenderman, Cecelia Shepherd, Hazel Keyes, and Lisa Carlson.

Sarajane Helm. "Miniature Masks." Masks are seen throughout history for all sorts of uses – theatrical, religious, decorative, and more.

Photo by Tim Thayer.

Kathleen Bolan. "Shinjitsu: Truth."

Photo by Chris Salek.

Chirs Salek. "Teapot Lady" vessel. It's always time for tea somewhere in the world!

Photo by Hema Hibbert.

Hema Hibbert. "Chinese Warrior" pendant and earrings.

Photo by Robert Diamante.

Lashonne Abel. "Old Sol" necklace.

Tools and Supplies

To Work With Polymer Clay, All You Truly

need is some clay, your hands, an oven thermometer, and an oven with a paper-lined pan for baking. However, there are many items that make the time spent much easier, more enjoyable, and the results more spectacular. Some of the most useful things in my studio setup include:

Tools and Supplies

- pasta roller(s)
- food processor
- work surface (ceramic tile, acrylic plate, marble slab, plastic placemat, etc.)
- flat knife (not serrated)
- assorted blades (Kato Nu-blade, Sculpey Super Slicer, microtome, ripple-fry cutter)
- decorative-edge scissors
- JASI Slicer
- X-acto or craft knife
- carving tools
- cookie and aspic cutters
- pointed wooden sticks (shish-kebob skewers, toothpicks)
- needle tool (bead reamer)
- acrylic rod roller or brayer
- rubber stamps and matrix plates
- molds
- texture tools
- wipe-out (rubber tip) sculpting tool
- plastic or metal scrapers
- clay gun and discs
- talcum powder or cornstarch
- ponce bag
- small makeup brush
- paintbrushes, both hair (in several sizes) and plastic bristle
- rags or old t-shirt

- acrylic paints
- markers and pencils
- mica and metallic powders and pigments
- metallic leaf
- Flecto Varathane
- jars, baskets, containers of all sorts
- premoistened wipes
- paper towels
- aloe vera gel
- vegetable oil
- stamp ink pads (Brilliance and Fabrico are both good brands for use with clay)
- glues, both PVA (white craft glue) and cyano-acrylate (Super Glue is one type)
- sandpaper, grits ranging from 60 to 2000
- emery boards
- Saran Wrap With Cling
- aluminum foil
- oven
- oven thermometer
- timer
- baking pans lined with white cardstock or paper
- polyester stuffing/batting
- cardboard pieces and toilet paper rolls
- oven mitts
- ironing board
- cooling rack

All tools you use with polymer clay should be used only with clay, never with food. Though certified as nontoxic art supplies, you still don't want to find cooked bits of hard clay in your next batch of cookies. Keep your clay tools separate from your normal cooking tools. In my home studio, this means a sort of artistic "keeping kosher," with one set of baking pans, food processor, garlic press, and so on, that is used only for clay. Another set is for the kitchen food preparations.

Although it is possible to use a regular home oven for baking clay (and most people do just that), always use it at separate times from food preparation. Don't bake the cookies and the beads in the same batch! If you bake frequently, consider getting a separate oven or toaster oven. Or you can use an aluminum foil "tent" over your items when baking. Large toaster ovens are actually much safer to use than the small ones because the heating element is farther away from the baking tray. If you line your pans with paper or cardstock, it helps protect your items from shiny spots. Some people bake on ceramic tiles to help conduct the heat evenly. I like to use small tufts of polyester stuffing or batting to support items like curved doll hands or flowers. Neither paper nor stuffing will burn at the suggested clay cooking temperatures. Cardboard tubes and small pieces of cardstock can also be bent, folded, and formed to make supports for items as needed. Other items useful in baking clay include ceramic items or small rocks that can be used as forms to shape the clay while baking. Always use a thermometer when baking. An ironing board makes a great place to put pans and hot items from the oven – the covers are meant to deal with heat!

Pasta Rollers and Food Processors

Pasta roller machines are made by several different manufacturers and can be found in cooking stores as well as from several clay suppliers. You can often find them at garage sales, flea markets, or on Internet auction sites. Use them for making clay conditioning much faster (and easier on the wrists) and for making even sheets of clay in a predetermined thickness.

Atlas machines are very good and quite easy to find. This brand is also marketed as a Marcato Atlas. It has seven or nine thickness settings. Another brand is the Pasta Queen, and it is much the same except the setting numbers are backwards from the Atlas. The Atlas starts with a thick #1 setting and goes to a paper thin #7 (or #9 on some machines), whereas a Pasta Queen has a wider aperture for the higher numbers. This is something to remember in classes or when following instructions. It is important to use evenly thick sheets when building precise canes or in making covered items, but the exact numeric measurement of the sheets is not crucial. (The sizes are likely to change over time if you force too thick a piece of clay through the opening, so do be careful.) Consistency while you work is a good thing but don't fret over the increments too much. If you are using a #1 sheet to build a cane, then stick with it throughout, and that should be exact enough.

The settings on my Marcato Atlas machine result in sheets of clay in the following thicknesses:

#1 = 1/8"
#2 = 3/32"
#3 = 1/16" (half as thick as #1)
#4 = 1/20"
#5 = 1/24"
#6 = 1/32" (half as thick as #3)
#7 = even thinner, but I couldn't measure it!

When using a pasta machine, slice clay from the block like pieces of cheese, or flatten the lumps from using a food processor into a pancake. Never try to force too thick a piece of clay through the rollers, as you can seriously bend parts and make rolling even sheets impossible. Clay can be run through the machine to condition it, or to blend and marble colors. When folding clay onto itself to run it through the machine again, just pinch the fold of the clay and insert it between the rollers. If you press the whole thing shut, it traps air bubbles and mixes them into the clay. Allow the two pieces to be put together by the action of the rollers themselves and save much bubble-popping labor later.

Start with the thickest setting first and progress to a thinner setting in steps. This avoids stressing the rollers and distorting the alignment, which will keep your machine in good working order and your settings even. It may be difficult to use a very thin setting if the clay is warm and overly pliable, so allow the clay to cool before putting it through the last time. You may also find it helpful to lightly powder the clay or the rollers, using a brush or a ponce bag. Some people place thin clay layers between sheets of parchment paper and roll it though for even thinner results. These extra-thin sheets are particularly useful when applying translucent clays.

Some people have several pasta rollers set up at the same time and keep one machine for white only, saving time on cleaning between colors.

Never get a pasta machine wet. Apply alcohol on a paper towel and clean the machine by running the towel through the opening at the narrowest setting or wipe it down with a soft cloth. If it's really messy, use a premoistened wipe to clean it after blotting the excess moisture from the wipe onto a paper towel.

You can purchase an electric motor for most pasta machines, which makes conditioning large amounts go very quickly. However, many people object to the noise level the motor creates. Use earplugs or baffles to protect your ears if you are exposed to a noisy motor for long periods of time.

Pasta machines often come with noodle cutter attachments, which can be very useful for making even strips of clay using raw or cooked sheets of clay.

Of course, it is possible to roll clay without a pasta machine. Many people use an acrylic rod or brayer for this. These rods (and acrylic sheets for work surfaces) can be purchased from some clay suppliers or found at sign-making shops. Look under "acrylic" and "plastic" to see what is near you. Shops often have bins of scrap pieces that are just right for clay purposes.

A food processor is particularly useful in conditioning very firm clays like Fimo or older clays that have hardened somewhat. It will also make short work of color mixing. Put small amounts in as the blades are whirling to avoid clumping and straining the motor (softer clays like Premo don't require this step as a usual part of conditioning). Whirl the clay in the processor. The clay is broken up and warmed at the same time. Don't leave it unattended and don't let it go too long or the clay can overheat. Very small amounts of vegetable oil, such as canola oil, can be added to further soften hard clays. Add a few drops at a time while pulsing the clay in the processor, and grind the clay to the size of coarse coffee grounds.

Blades

When working with polymer clay, you will need several blades, including some interesting ones such as the wavy-fry cutter (also known as a ripple blade). Some, like microtome blades, are designed to slice tissue samples for biopsy tests and all of them are extremely sharp. Use caution with blades and don't let them float around unsecured. I keep mine in place with business card sized magnets mounted on the inside lid of my tool kit.

You can make a carry case for blades by using two flat pieces of clay, a bit larger than your blades. Glue a binding of leather to join them like a book, or poke holes along the sides and lace them together. Put a strip of magnet along the top and bottom of each side and place the blades on the magnets before closing the carrier. This makes them much safer to transport.

Use ripple blades in some kinds of mokume gane and layered techniques. Use others like the microtome, Kato Nu-Blade, or Sculpey Super Slicer to cut through blocks of clay or to make delicate cane slices. For making very even and exactly repeatable cuts, especially from very wide canes, use a JASI slicer. Designed by Judith Skinner, this has a blue steel blade and cuts amazingly precise pieces.

An X-acto knife is highly useful in making detailed and intricate cuts, and a flat blade knife (not serrated) is great for sliding under pieces to remove them from the work surface. Cutting wheels, pizza cutters, and decorative-edge scissors can also be used to cut clay.

Texture Tools

Once you begin working with polymer clay, you will quickly notice its versatility, and that just about everything is a potential tool to use with the clay. Rubber stamps, sewing tools, art supplies, and bits and pieces from every other craft or art medium – all can be wonderfully useful. A trip to the supermarket or hardware store can be a whole new experience when you are looking with clay in mind. A comb meant for pets or a baby comb can become texture tools, and so can the end of a ballpoint pen when the ink cartridge is removed (save the little spring too – it makes an interesting texture).

Decorative screw heads, even the serrated edge from a box of aluminum foil, can add to your texture repertoire. A trip to the thrift store can add wonderful finds. An old grater has several different textures on it. Or look for candy molds or old cut/pressed glass pieces, or buttons on clothing. There are textures and tools everywhere but you have to learn to see them for what they can be as well as for what they are. Crumpled aluminum foil, lace, fabric, seashells, even rough rocks or sandpaper can be used to create interesting surfaces on clay.

Molds, Cutters, Etc.

I particularly like to collect small cookie cutters and candy molds. You can often find these on sale after the holidays at craft and hobby stores. There is a huge variety of aspic-type cutters available, including triangles, stars, hearts, clubs, spades, diamonds, and many other shapes. Aspic cutters are like miniature cookie cutters – shaped metal that is sharp on one side with an open top and bottom. I also like Kemper cutters – small brass cutters with plungers. Off The Beaten Path (see Sources, page 143) carries an incredible collection of cookie cutters at reasonable prices, including butterflies, snowflakes, alphabets, animals, flowers, leaves, and much more. I used several in the clay projects in this book.

Another source of shapes and textures are Shadex Scratch-Art sheets. These are available from the Clay Factory in a wide variety of styles (see Sources, page 143). These 8-1/2" x 11" acrylic sheets are impressed with many kinds of images and are made so the designs protrude on one side of the sheet and go in on the other, giving you two options for each sheet. They are very lightweight and slippery and I have found it easier to cut them into smaller sections (most are repeat designs and easily cut into quarters with scissors or a paper cutter) and punch a hole in one corner of each. Then I put a set together on a metal circle clip or ring binder. I cut

Small cookie cutter sets and Kemper tool sets.

Letter cutters can be used to spell out anything. Use them with plain or decorated clay.

Shapelets acrylic templates from Polyform.

Clay can be pressed into Shadex texture sheets. Here tiny Beedz fill the crevices.

pictures of the designs out of the Clay Factory's catalog and mount them on a sheet of cardstock that I put on the circle clip to show how each design looks when used.

A piece of the sheet can be used as is or removed from the circle clip and passed through the pasta roller with a sheet of clay. After use, it is important to clean the sheets or the clay residue will interact with the sheet and spoil it for future use.

The Shadex snowflake design shown here was used to impress the clay and tiny glass Beedz (which have no holes) were used to fill the indentations after baking. I used Flecto Varathane to hold them in place (it works as a glue as well as a finish).

Small hole-less glass balls, such as Beedz, can also be used to embellish the surface of polymer clay beads. Roll a pierced ball of clay in a small amount of the Beedz, then roll the ball carefully in the palm of your hands to firmly embed the pieces in the clay. Don't push them too far in or you will lose the light-catching effect of the glass. It is very important to use Beedz away from other clays and your pasta roller – do it over a container or box lid (and capture the excess for use another time) rather than over your normal work surface. These tiny balls scatter easily and are hard to see and if you roll a piece of clay containing these or seed beads through the pasta roller, you can permanently indent the rollers, marking your future clay sheets forever.

Clay sheets can also be cut into very interesting shapes using a knife and cutting freehand, or by using Shapelets sets produced by Polyform. These acrylic templates come in a variety of designs and can be cut out with an X-Acto knife to create beautiful shapes in clay that are easily and exactly repeatable. Pieces can be imprinted or textured before or after cutting, and cut pieces can be layered for a very cleanly finished look.

Tamila Darling's new Darling Designer Discs, meant for use with a clay gun, hold many possible delights for polymer clay users. These small discs have intricately cut shapes, and

Polymer clay beads rolled in Beedz glass and metallic balls.

when used correctly, allow you to extrude an astounding variety of shapes ranging from the simple to the very complex. Available in geometric and other shapes such as snowflakes, leaves, butterflies, and more, these can be used in a number of ways. Extruded shapes can be used in building canes or as "seam binding" for use in mosaics and sculptures to hide raw joins. Extruded lengths of the clay can be baked and sliced while still warm. These can even be pierced with a tiny pin drill to make the most amazing little beads! It is vital that you follow the package directions exactly for good results. To maintain your discs for future use, clean them immediately after contact with polymer clay.

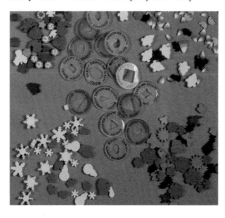

Simply Darling Designer Discs for use with a clay gun, plus extrusions that have been baked and sliced.

Rubber Stamps

Another tool that's dear to my heart is the rubber stamp. You can use commercially available stamps or make your own. When purchasing a commercial stamp, look for one with that will penetrate deeply into the clay, with bold lines rather than very fine ones. This type of stamp will make a better impression in the clay when used as a press mold, and will form a clearer image when used with powders or inks. You can wet the stamp with aloe vera, then apply powders to transfer the image cleanly onto clay. Bake to help set the powders before applying any liquid clays or other finishing glazes.

Remember that commercial stamps are meant for your individual use only, not for professional use. This means that while you are free to use them for your own decorative items, they are not meant to make things to sell. If you wish to make items to market, you must use stamps from a company with an "angel policy" or you will violate copyright laws. An angel policy means that the artist whose design is used in the rubber stamp has given permission for the limited use of that design. Most require that you do not make copies of the stamps themselves and that the items you make using the stamps are handmade and created in small batches, not mechanically reproduced in quantity. Many artists (including me) license their art for use by rubber stamp manufacturers but still retain the copyright to their designs. I design stamps for Uptown Design Co. (see Sources, page 143), who has an angel policy for many of their designs. When in doubt about a design's status, ask. Uptown Design Co. stamps are used throughout this book and are listed by title and number. I like them because not only is it morally and legally okay to use these designs in your work, but the stamps themselves are very well made. The rubber is deeply etched and quite hard, giving more resistance when used with clay. The company carries an extensive line of designs available at retail stores and online.

Hard rubber stamps will not interact quickly with polymer clay as do acrylic or foam rubber stamps. Use a water-based rubber stamp cleanser after repeated use or you may clog the details with clay buildup. Store stamps out of direct sunlight and heat.

You can carve your own stamps from erasers or from polymer clay, especially the more flexible clays. Or you can have stamps made from your own drawings or copyright-free sources of art such as those found in the Dover Pictorial Archive series (see Sources, page 143). Up to 10 images from a single Dover source so designated can be used without further permission.

These stamps are made through a company called Ready Stamps in San Diego (see Sources, page 143). They are a sheltered workshop division of the United Cerebral Palsy Assoc. of America, and many office supply companies that "make" stamps actually have them produced through Ready Stamps. They offer a very sweet deal to artists: you can get uncut and unmounted sheets of rubber stamps made from your original designs or copyright-free designs, and if you ask when you order, you can also get the plate and matrix from which it was made. Here's how it works.

Choose or create the artwork. You can use original drawings in pen and ink, computer graphic printouts, your company name, your logo, a signature, or designs from many clip art sources and from books such as the Dover Pictorial Archive Series. Many of the clip art designs in computer software are actually from the Dover Pictorial Archive. You'll begin to recognize them after you've looked at a few of these wonderful books. These designs are seen everywhere in advertising and newsletters. In the example shown, I used eight images from Dover's Traditional Stencil Designs from India by Pradumna and Rosalba Tana. I scanned the images from my purchased book rather than cut them out (I don't advocate cutting up books). In addition to keeping my book intact, scanning and importing the images into my computer allows me to change the image size and to reverse it into negative form. On a 9" x 7" sheet, I can paste printouts of the images in different scales and juxtapositions. This still counts as "under 10" images. (I called Dover and specifically asked and also got permission to show them in this book. When in doubt, ask.)

Don't use copyright-protected material that is not drawn by you unless you have specific permission. This includes recognizable cartoon characters originally drawn by someone else. (For more detailed and current information about copyright laws, consult the local library, a copyright lawyer, or the Internet. It comes down to this – an artist controls the right to limit any copied use of their artwork.) Any use of someone else's work, unless it is with their specific permission or the work is old enough to be in the public domain, is not only illegal, it is wrong, whether you are caught or not.

Use a 9" x 7" rectangle on a sheet of clean white paper or cardstock. Cut out the drawn or photocopied images and arrange them inside the rectangle, allowing a little room between the design elements so they can be cut apart when they are in rubber form. Try cutting squares or strips of images with interesting "texture" patterns. Use images with clear detail and sharp contrast. Avoid thin lines and large dark areas. When satisfied with your designs, glue them in place (I use a glue stick). Leave

Black and white artwork becomes the matrix, acrylic, and rubber sheet from Ready Stamps.

enough room between designs for scissors, but don't place them too far apart. The juxtaposition of designs can be very useful in the matrix.

When mailing, sandwich the artwork between two sheets of cardboard so it doesn't wrinkle or smudge. Every mark will be reproduced when the stamps are made.

Remember to specify "plate," "matrix," and "rubber" when you order. Some people don't use all three, but they are wonderful tools for making texture and pattern in pressed paper or polymer clay. I actually use the matrix more often than the rubber. The rubber can be rolled with a sheet of clay through the widest opening of a pasta roller for especially good detail. I usually leave my stamps unmounted for versatility's sake.

Miscellaneous

In almost two decades of working with polymer clay, I have gathered many interesting bits and pieces, products, and powders. I have found wonderful containers (bottles, jars, and more) at American Science and Surplus (see Sources, page 143). One of my favorites is an aluminum box with 20 small cylindrical containers originally meant for gemstones. The glass tops on the small pots make it easy to view the contents and I have filled up three sets with all sorts of little treasures. These sets fit neatly inside a metal lunchbox. I also have several flat boxes that originally held mints, and I keep one to hold a ponce bag filled with powder and a small makeup brush. Using the ponce bag and the brush, large or small areas can be powdered to make molds or impressions.

To make a ponce bag, cut a 6" circle of woven fabric. Pour a few spoonfuls of talcum powder or cornstarch in the center, bring up the outside edges of the cloth to form a pouch, and tie it above the powder with a rubber band or string. Trim excess fabric if needed. Use the bag by lightly dragging it across the surface you wish to powder. Small amounts of the powder will come out over time (that is the function, after all!) so keep the bag in a container or dish when it's not in use. The powder that comes out in the box is just the right amount for dipping a small makeup brush to powder deeply carved or highly dimensional objects. When I carry this with a piece of Super Elasticlay or other soft polymer clay, I am ready to make molds anywhere I find an intriguing surface. (Remember to ask permission before taking molds of someone's doorknob, silverware, etc., and always wipe off the surface with a soft cloth afterwards.)

Sometimes you will want a perfectly smooth surface rather than a textured one. My well-moisturized fingers are still my favorite tools for smoothing, but I also use a rubber tipped tool with a chisel shape on one end and a rounded point on the other. This is good for smoothing tiny crevices as well as for shaping flower petals. A soft-hair paintbrush can be used to smooth small areas of rough clay before baking. After baking, use an emery board to smooth the outside edges of a piece. Also use sandpaper to smooth rough areas.

Polymer related goodies. The clay and tools fit in a decorated toolbox that was originally meant to hold lunch.

For general sanding, start with a lower number (rougher) grit and move up to a higher number, working to the paper that is almost smooth. This is sometimes called "wet/dry" sandpaper or automotive finish paper.

Carving tools, small drills, and other tools can be used to shape polymer clay before or after baking. Hand drills or small electrical drills can be used to pierce beads after baking, or use a needle tool or

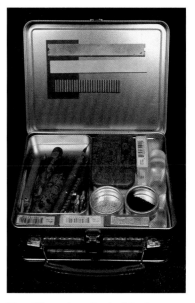

Now it's my travel set of tools.

bead reamer to poke holes in raw clay. Wire, glass, and other items can be decorative elements in clay works, and the tools for using them often find their way into my studio (pliers, wire cutters, etc. can be very handy). In fact, be prepared for a steady migration of useful things into your clay work area.

Tile, glass, marble, acrylic sheets, Formica, Masonite, or Melamine make smooth and portable work surfaces that are easy to use and clean. Most are available at hardware stores, often sold as shelving. Ceramic and stone floor tiles are also good work surfaces. Banquet tables make a strong worktable with the added benefit of being sturdy enough to hold the clamp of a pasta roller. A solid work surface such as an acrylic sheet or ceramic tile helps protect the tabletop from cuts and damage from the raw clay (never leave clay on a fine wood surface). A clear acrylic sheet is a particularly good work surface because you can place it over a measuring grid and be able to see the size and straight lines and angles.

Polymer Basics

PREPARING POLYMER CLAY FOR USE

Conditioning

Acrylic sheets and acrylic rods for rolling the clay can be found at shops that fabricate signs for businesses. Look in the business listings under "plastics," "acrylics," or "signs." Some polymer clay suppliers now carry these items as well.

Polymer clays, like earth clays, must be conditioned and prepared for use. Even though some brands are already quite soft, for best results you must still prepare the clay. This aligns the molecules and makes the final piece much stronger.

Always start with very clean hands and fingernails because the clay will pick up any dirt or natural oils. This is especially apparent with white and light colors. (Premoistened wipes are great for polymer cleanup jobs and don't dry out your hands.)

Clean your work surface, too, and remember that clays will dull or even remove the finish from a fine wood surface.

To condition clay, slice and chop it with a blade or with a processor. If conditioning by hand, roll the clay into a snake, ball it up, and roll it out again. Do this many times.

If conditioning with a pasta machine, flatten the clay into a pancake less than 3/8" thick and put it through a pasta roller at the widest setting (#1 on Atlas machines). This produces a sheet or "tongue" of clay. Fold this in half lengthwise, but don't press the two halves together along their length (that traps air bubbles). Place the fold between the rollers and allow it to press together by itself as you pass it through. Repeat the process. Folds should always go into the roller first, or along the side of the piece being rolled. If the fold is at the top, air will be trapped. Put the clay through several times. If the clay crumbles, roll it back into a snake and start over. If mixing colors, you may find it goes faster if you put the clay through a smaller opening after a few passes. Move through the settings, going from #1 to #2 to #3 in sequence to avoid stressing the openings. Colors are properly conditioned when you have passed it through enough times to completely blend two colors into a new one, perhaps one or two dozen times.

If your clay is very hard, soften it by using a food processor with the chopping blade. Add a few drops of vegetable oil while using the processor. Don't pour the oil directly from the bottle into the processor. Instead, pour a few drops into the cap or a spoon, then add it to the clay. Run the food processor in short bursts, and don't leave it unattended, as the clay will heat during use. This heating is helpful in small doses, but overheating will start to cook the clay. If you are conditioning the clay by hand, add small amounts of oil by lightly coating your hands with oil and continuing to work the clay.

You can also soften clay by adding transparent clay, which is softer than most colored clays and will add plasticiser to the hard clay. Or you can purchase a product called Fimo Mix Quick that is very helpful for softening hard clay because it contains even more plasticiser than translucent clay.

If your clay is hard as a rock, try processing it with a processor or by hand, then put it in a plastic sandwich bag or wrap it in plastic wrap and leave it overnight. This allows the active ingredients to "travel" and helps to permeate the old clay with new plasticiser. Then flatten the clay and condition it as usual. It takes a little extra effort, but most old clays can be revitalized in this manner. However, if the clay is not just old, but partially baked, it may not be possible to soften it. On the rare occasion that this happens, I chop the clay in a food processor and use the bits as rocklike inclusions if the color is appropriate. If not, I add a little gold, silver, or copper powder to the chopped bits in the bowl of the processor and whirl it again. I pour the resulting "nuggets" on a baking pan, spread them lightly, and bake. These can be used as inclusions in soft clay or can be glued in place as is (they look just like raw metal nuggets). You can also make miniature "rocks" and "pebbles" in this fashion (leaving out the metal powders), which can be wonderfully useful with miniature displays.

If your clay is too soft, it can be made more workable by "wicking" or "leaching" excess plasticiser from the clay. To do this, roll the clay into sheets and place the sheets between two pieces of paper. The oily film that soaks into the paper is the plasticiser, a chemical solvent, and should be disposed of safely in the trash. However, recent evidence suggests that wicking the clay also removes important stabilizers and can result in less structural integrity in the final piece.

Chunks of softer clay, especially Premo and Cernit, can cause the blade to stick, and I generally don't use a processor with these. A processor is not really needed for softer clays. If you use one to mix clay, be ready to turn the unit off if the blade sticks, to save the motor.

Clays that have already been conditioned can be re-chopped to achieve very realistic mottled stone effects. Different consistencies of clay can also be mixed to find a happier medium. When mixing old hard clay and new soft clay, a messy sort of shredding takes place. It will eventually all work together, but the partially mixed clay can be used to create very interesting effects as the clay is put through the pasta roller. Sometimes I even do this on purpose! Place a thin sheet of old clay (if you don't have any, leave some clay uncovered for a week) on top of a thicker slab of softer clay in a different color, then roll it down to pancake thickness and put it through the pasta roller on the widest setting. As it starts to break up, fold the clay tongue so that an interesting-looking patch is on top. When put through the rollers again it will start to look like watercolor splotches, or stone, or even tortoiseshell if done with the right colors. Translucent clay added to the mix creates interesting depths and mixes. If the sheet gets too thin, pad it with more clay or just keep folding what you have, keeping the part you like on top. I stumbled on this technique by accident and I call it one of those "I meant to do that" artistic techniques. Many times what seems to be a mistake is actually the beginning of a new effect. When people ask, "How did you do that?" I smile and say, "Oh, it's a special technique. I meant to do that!"

If you have wrist or hand strength problems or are working with large quantities of clay, it's helpful to use a pasta roller to mechanically compress and thus condition the clay. This has the added advantage of rolling the clay into even sheets of adjustable thickness.

Adjusting and Mixing Colors

Mixing colors makes it possible to personalize the color range to your exact preference. Everyone sees color

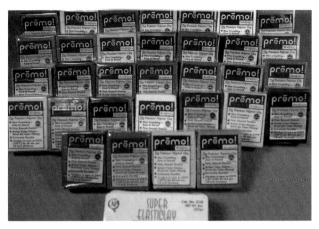

The color range of Premo, plus Super Elasticlay.

differently, and there are so many variations of shade, hue, tone, and tint. Colors can be mixed with translucent or white as a base, or pearl white for shimmering effects that are caused by the mica in the clay.

Add a little white clay to keep any color from darkening when baked, which is more of a problem with some colors and clays than others. More opaque clays (which had some white added in the manufacturing process) do not darken as much as clays with a transparent base.

I add black to much of my clay palette to "sadden" or tone down the intensity of the colors. I prefer muted shades or vibrant colors that are not necessarily bright. If you like bright, try adding fluorescent colors to your mixes. Violet and fluorescent pink make the most wonderful purples. Adding small amounts of fluorescent colors can really perk things up.

Using a pasta roller makes color blending fast and easy. Or you can do color blending by hand by rolling and kneading two or more colors of clay until they blend. Partial blending is used for a marbled effect, but individual colors should be conditioned first, as continued kneading will result in a solid color or shade that differs from the original colors.

Color Recipes

Marie Segal is an accomplished polymer clay artist who not only runs the Clay Factory (see Sources, page 143) with her husband Howard, but was also instrumental in choosing the colors used in manufacturing Premo clay. Working closely with the chemists at Polyform, the makers of Premo, Sculpey, and Elasticlay, she advocated the use of the pigment and color names traditionally used in oil paints, so that color mixing could be standardized. Marie graciously shared the recipes for all the color mixes shown in her season palettes (see page 20). All use Premo clay.

To use her recipe measurements, divide each block of clay into four equal parts, or use a cutter and sheets of clay to mix smaller amounts. To do this, use pieces made with any one cutter and clay sheets of even thickness to be your equal parts.

Spring

Strawberry Smoothie
12 pt. White
1 pt. Alizarin Crimson
4 pt. Fuchsia

Salmon
7 pt. White
1 pt. Orange
1 pt. Fuchsia

Lemon Pie
3 pt. White
1 pt. Cadmium Yellow

Key Lime Pie
7 pt. White
1 pt. Sap Green

Mint
13 pt. White
3 pt. Green
1 pt. Ultramarine Blue

Sky
3 pt. White
1 pt. Ultramarine Blue
4 pt. Turquoise

Lilac
7 pt. White
2 pt. Fuchsia
1 pt. Ultramarine Blue

Summer

Raspberry
12 pt. Fuchsia
1 pt. White

Candied Apple
8 pt. Cadmium Red
2 pt. Fuchsia
1 pt. White

Tangerine
7 pt. Orange
1 pt. White
1 pt. Zinc Yellow

Banana
6 pt. Zinc Yellow
2 pt. White

Key Lime
10 pt. Fluorescent Green
2 pt. Zinc Yellow
3 pt. White

Blue Curaco
10 pt. Turquoise
1 pt. Pearl Blue
2 pt. White

Grape
3 pt. Ultramarine Blue
3 pt. Fuchsia
1 pt. White

Fall

Violet Gold
2 pt. Violet
1 pt. Gold

Copper
1 pt. Alizarin Crimson
1 pt. Gold

Golden Rose
2 pt. Fuchsia
1 pt. Gold

Pumpkin Gold
2 pt. Orange
1 pt. Gold

Bright Gold
3 pt. Gold
1 pt. Silver

Bronze
3 pt. Gold
1 pt. Black

Antique Bronze
1 pt. Ultramarine Blue
1 pt. Gold

Brown Bronze
4 pt. Burnt Umber
1 pt. Gold

Green Gold
2 pt. Green
1 pt. Gold

Avocado Gold
11 pt. Ultramarine Blue
1 pt. Green
1 pt. Gold

Jade
2 pt. Pearl Green
1 pt. Gold

Verdi Gris
2 pt. Turquoise
1 pt. Gold

Blue Bronze
5 pt. Ultramarine Blue
1 pt. Gold

Golden Plum
2 pt. Ultramarine
2 pt. Fuchsia
1 pt. Gold

Winter

Carmine
2 pt. Fuchsia
1 pt. Alizarin Crimson

Hyacinth
3 pt. Orange
1 pt. Gold

Light Bronze
1 pt. Gold
1 pt. Silver

Hunter Green
2 pt. Pearl Green
1 pt. Black

Peacock
2 pt. Pearl Green
1 pt. Ultramarine Blue

Steel Blue
2 pt. Ultramarine Blue
1 pt. Silver

Amethyst
2 pt. Fuchsia
1 pt. Ultramarine Blue
1 pt. Pearl White

Graphite
1 pt. Pearl White
1 pt. Black

Recipes courtesy of Marie Segal.

A good way to keep track of your color blends is to make a bead from every color you mix. Save and string them to see your palette. These blends are all Premo pearlized clays mixed with Pearl White or Gold as a base.

Recording Color Results

Keep a record of mixed colors on recipe cards or by making a single bead from each color. When strung, these beads give you instant reference points for the colors you use most. Or roll out a sheet of clay and use a small cutter to make a tile of each color sample. After baking, these chips can be glued to a recipe card or used in a mosaic. Glue them all to a sheet of cardstock for easy comparison or reference, or leave them separate and use them to check colors when thinking of designs. By putting colors close to each other on a sheet of paper, you can readily see how they look together.

I called on Judith Skinner, Leigh Ross, and Marie Segal to join me in preparing our own seasonal palettes. Each of us made a collection of color chips using Kemper cutters and the clays we use most frequently. Though they span the rainbow, these personal palettes do show areas of favoritism from each artist. Try it and see where your preferences fall.

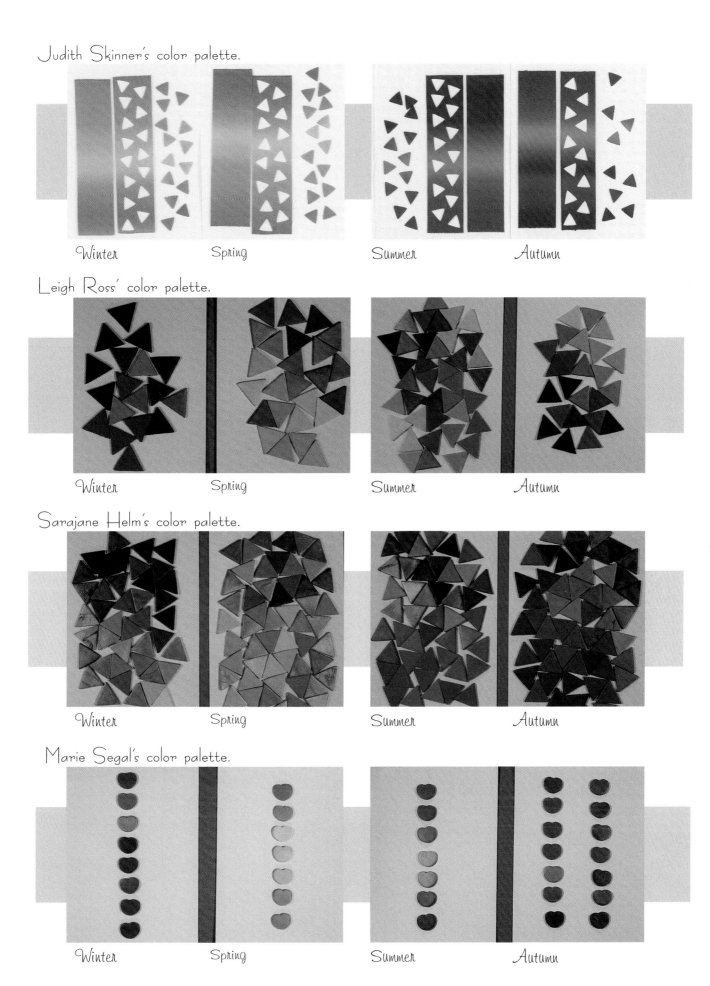

Judith Skinner's color palette.

Winter   Spring   Summer   Autumn

Leigh Ross' color palette.

Winter   Spring   Summer   Autumn

Sarajane Helm's color palette.

Winter   Spring   Summer   Autumn

Marie Segal's color palette.

Winter   Spring   Summer   Autumn

Storing Unbaked Clay

Clays can be conditioned and stored until you are ready to use them. If properly kept, they will not dry out or harden unless they are heated. I prepare clays in quantity and wrap the large chunks in plastic wrap, then break off pieces as needed, or I leave them all together on a metal cookie sheet and cover it with plastic wrap. A quick roll in my hands to warm the clay is usually all that's needed when I'm ready to begin. I also use sheets of plastic wrap to cover work in progress if I need to leave it for any length of time, and to wrap cane lengths.

Not all plastics will work together. Saran With Cling is compatible with polymer clay. You need to be alert when using new products with clay. If there's any melting over time, it's a sign that the chemicals from one plastic are eating the other, and those plastics are not compatible. Once you find something that works, stick with it.

Plastic wrap helps keep raw clay soft and workable (I have some canes that are six years old that are fine). Cover works in progress to keep dust, pet hair, and other debris in the air from settling on the clay. It is far easier to protect a piece than it is to clean it up afterwards. I also protect my clays from exposure to UV light by keeping canes in a covered box, and blocks of unopened clay in a dresser drawer. Don't keep clay on a windowsill in direct light! Clay begins to cure at 110°, so watch where you store it. Don't leave it in the car or on top of an appliance.

Working With Add-Ins and Powders

As if a full range of color choices, and matte, metallic, and pearl finishes aren't enough, many other things can also be added to the clays for visual interest! Dried spices or vegetable matter, pigments, and powders can all be worked into the clay. PearlEx powders are particularly useful because they are mica based and have a wide range of metallic and reflective colors. Fimo Bronzepulver and other metallic powders are made with powdered aluminum and give the most clearly defined image when stamping, but require more care and caution in use.

To make very sure you don't breathe in any of these powders, wear a respirator or filter mask when working with them. Even talcum powder, used as a mold release, contains ground rock with a small amount of naturally occurring asbestos, so get in the habit of working with powders in a slow and unhurried manner so as not to produce clouds of it in the air. If there is a spill, wait until the dust settles, then clean it up with a damp paper towel. I use scented talcum powder and if I can smell it I know I am flinging it around too hard – time for the filter mask.

Using a brush to apply powders seems to be one of the easiest ways to work up a cloud of it, and the glinting dust motes in the air are pretty but undesirable. I apply powders in other ways, lightly using a ponce bag for talc, and using my index finger to apply metallic powders. I have

Beedz, Inclusions, PearlEx powders, and other items for use with clay fit nicely inside these little round containers that come in their own box, from American Science and Surplus. Blades stay put on a magnet.

been assured that the aluminum is too big a molecule to easily get through the skin, which works quite well at its barrier job. Not so in your lungs. The biggest danger from aluminum comes when it is breathed (unless metal allergies are present – then it is a good idea to stay away from the Bronzepulvers completely). Always wash your hands immediately after using powder so you don't accidentally get it in your eyes or elsewhere. Clean hands also keep the rest of the clay in your studio uncontaminated. I keep a pre-moistened wipe handy to keep my hands clean.

Powder mixed directly into the clay can create some very beautiful effects. Stamped pieces that didn't turn out quite right can be wadded back up with powder dispersed into the clay. At first in a localized swirl, the powder moves through the entire mass as you continue to work the clay. The more translucent the clay, the more the powders and other inclusions seem to float. You can create opalescent effects, especially when you buff translucent clays to a high sheen. Glitter, confetti, fibers, and other items can be used on top or mixed into polymer clays. So can some stamp embossing powders and some dyes. Very fine glitters labeled "micro-crystalline" are particularly effective. Some brands can melt, though, so always do a test piece before making up a large batch. Metallic foils or leaf can be used to spectacular effect, especially with translucent clays.

Baking Times and Temperatures

As stated previously, it is possible to use a regular home oven for baking clay (and most people do just that). For safety's sake, always bake clay at a different time than baking food. Don't bake food and clay in the same batch! If you bake clay frequently, consider getting a separate oven or toaster oven. Or use an aluminum foil "tent" over your clay items when baking.

The most important thing to remember about using polymer clays safely is to not overheat the clay. Each brand specifies times and temperatures that work best with that clay. Pieces are baked in a home oven (never a microwave) or large toaster oven at temperatures ranging from 250°F to 300°F. Most small projects require 20 to 40 minutes of baking in a 260°F to 275°F oven. There are exceptions to this – light colors such as transparent, flesh, porcelain, white, and glow-in-the-darks are best baked at 260°F for 30 minutes, and it's easy to overbake so watch the clock. These darken as they cook longer. You can rebake pieces as often as necessary, adding more clay at each stage, and you can reheat items to make them flexible or softer to cut or carve.

Watch out for yellowing or melting. This is not a desirable outcome and indicates a too-high temperature. Although polymer clays must be heated to the proper temperature to polymerize (harden), burning begins at 350°F and at higher temperatures toxic fumes are released. This is true of all plastics, and is easy to avoid by keeping watch over your oven thermostat. Most ovens are off by a number of degrees so it is very important to purchase an oven thermometer and test the various areas in your oven. Some have corners or spots that are 10°F to 75°F warmer. Small toaster ovens are especially variable, and the temperature nearest the heating coil can burn the clay while other parts of the oven don't get hot enough to fully cure it. Also, oven temperatures may go much higher than you think when preheating, so check yours before starting anything in a cold oven. I use a large Toastmaster Platinum brand convection toaster oven and occasionally a home oven for very large pieces. I get best results by being careful. I preheat the oven before use and consistently use a thermometer. A timer helps keep me from forgetting any batches that are baking while I tend to other things.

Slight smoking from the clay may occur around 300°F but this is not the same as the smoke from burning clay. Still, clay should never be heated any higher than this. The results of actually burning the clay include blackening and very dark noxious smoke that will irritate and can damage your soft tissues (eyes, nose, and lungs). If you accidentally overheat your oven load and noxious fumes are released, turn off the oven, open the windows and doors, and air out the place. Don't leave a tray of clay in the oven to cool and forget it when you or someone else turns on the oven for dinner (this is the biggest reason to use a different oven for clay). After such an incident, wipe down the inside of your cooled oven with a warm soapy washcloth and again with plain water. Then wash the rag out or dispose of it.

Always work in a well-ventilated area. Use an accurate oven temperature gauge. These are inexpensive and are available at grocery stores and most kitchen departments.

Buffing and Sanding

Clay can be sanded and buffed after baking. Different grits of sandpaper are required for various parts of the task. Use 100-grit just for a moment or two to begin sanding very rough clay surfaces, or for sanding away the raised tops of baked pieces in mica shift techniques. This grit can also be used to scratch wood grain lines in baked pieces.

When sanding, start with clay that has been stroked with your finger to remove fingerprints prior to baking. (I call this "petting" and it saves hours of sanding.) Then use sandpaper on the baked and cooled clay to further smooth it. Use light, smooth strokes in one direction, not in circles. Sand all over the surface, then switch to a higher number, finer grit sandpaper. I use grits of 600, 1200, and 2000. These higher numbers look like smooth gray paper and can be used wet or dry. I do all sanding with wet sandpaper to really smooth the surface and give it the start of a sheen. (Using it wet also reduces the amount of dust in the air.) You should only have to sand with each grit of paper for a few moments before going on to the next. Sanding will remove the very top layer of clay to eliminate smudges and reveal clearer patterns of cane work, or just to give a soft polish to the clay.

After sanding comes buffing, which is done with a cloth (denim is a good choice). Many people use a buffing wheel with a muslin disc, and with patience and careful work can achieve a glassy shine and lovely finish. Translucent clays can be made almost transparent with the use of thin layers and much sanding and buffing. I don't use a buffer very often, preferring to use Flecto Varathane to get a shiny finish, as I use a lot of powders and foils, and these would be sanded away with sandpaper or buffing. If you do use machines for sanding or buffing, be sure to wear eye safety goggles and use a filter mask (available at the hardware store) so as not to breathe the dust.

Metallic and pearl clays also benefit greatly from sanding and buffing. Because these clays contain mica, displacement effects can be used by impressing the clays, then slicing the raised portions of the raw clay or sanding away the raised portions of the baked clay. The original design will be visible in the layers of mica within the clay. This technique can be very beautiful when done carefully. Sanding and buffing bring out the real beauty in these pieces. You can also use the cutoff bits to decorate other items, but be careful – it's easy to cut too deeply and mar the original impression.

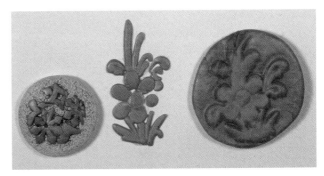

Raised portions sliced from gold clay and applied to other pieces.

OTHER FINISHES

When using powders in a surface application such as rubber stamping or with exposed metallic foils, a protective covering must be added after the clay is baked. Inclusions inside clay are protected by the clay itself, but if the cut edges of metal foils are in contact with air and moisture, they can tarnish and stain the clay long after baking. When sealed correctly, the less expensive composition leaf is very suitable for polymer clay and retains its beauty for years. Aluminum leaf can be used in place of silver, and gold composition leaf is much less expensive than 22K gold leaf. Copper is also available, and so are many colored types, with red, black, green, and blue anodized effects that are vivid and beautiful.

The best product I have found for use as a polymer clay finish is available at many hardware stores. The full name is Flecto Varathane Diamond Wood Finish (Interior). Although the company was recently purchased by the same corporation that owns Rustoleum, I have been assured that the Flecto Varathane formula will remain the same. It is water-based and easy to apply with a brush, and you can clean up with soap and water. It is compatible with the clay and shows no changes or degradation after 12 years of my testing (and it doesn't smell bad).

Flecto Varathane has what they call "IPN" or Interpenetrating Network and it goes into the clay itself. This is particularly helpful when using it with foils, powders, and paints. Its interpenetrating quality really helps with adhesion of these over long-term wear.

Flecto Varathane is available in gloss, semi-gloss, and satin, terms that refer to the degree of shine present when it dries. I recently tried the satin and was able to see the difference between it and gloss, though it was still shinier than unglazed clay.

I buy Flecto in quart cans, fill a clean jar, and work from the jar. This protects the bulk of the Flecto from contamination or hardening. Flecto Varathane seems to dry out faster when mixed with paints or powders, so I generally mix as much stain as I need immediately rather than try to keep it fresh for months.

Six tablespoons of varathane fills one three-ounce plastic container about half full. To minimize streaking and air bubbles, use a soft-hair paintbrush to apply surface coatings. If the lid of the jar you are using to store the varathane becomes cemented in place, run it under hot water for a few minutes. Prevent this by keeping the jar rim and lid clean and dry. Also avoid wiping your brush against the side of the jar, as this adds air bubbles and gets the jar messy.

Paints or pigments mixed in high concentration with varathane can be used to fill indents in baked clay. They look remarkably like enamel when buffed lightly with a polishing cloth (denim or t-shirts make good buffing cloths).

Flecto Varathane can be rebaked if necessary. In fact, the heat seems to fill in tiny brush strokes and set the glaze when rebaked. When baking Flecto, keep the temperature around 225°F (less than for baking the clay) and don't heat for very long – 10 minutes or less. I rebake most often not because I want to affect the Flecto, but because beads sometimes get stuck on the bamboo skewers and reheating lets me remove them easily. Flecto can also be used in mosaics like a glue to hold small pieces in place (it certainly works on the beads and skewers).

You can make stains for use on baked clay by mixing Flecto Varathane with pigments, powders, and acrylic paints. Stains typically have far less pigment in suspension than paints. Stains are usually applied then wiped off the surface with a soft cloth to remove the excess while still wet, leaving stain only in recessed areas. Use cheap plastic bristle brushes to apply stains so you can scrub and push the stain into all nooks and crevices without damaging an expensive brush. Sometimes you will need to apply several coats of stain to build up a good effect. Do this in steps, applying a thin coat and letting it dry completely before applying the next thin coat. One too-thick coat is not as effective and may even mark the clay in ways you don't like.

Use appropriate colored stains for each kind of clay base, for various effects. Shown are red, terra cotta, ochre, medium, dark, and gold.

Left. Stains made with Flecto Varathane as a base.

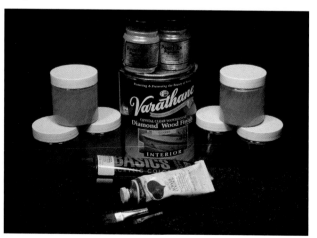

Stain Recipes

Dark Stain
6 T varathane
1 t black acrylic paint
1 t Sunset Gold PearlEx powder
This one is particularly useful on darker clays such as red or ochre when making faux cinnabar, coral, or bone.

Medium Stain
6 T varathane
1/2 t black acrylic paint
1/4 t Super Bronze PearlEx powder
Best for use on lighter clays and for making faux ivory.

Terra Cotta Stain
6 T varathane
1 t burnt sienna acrylic paint
Very good on lighter colors or on black. Useful in combination on faux ivory or bone.

Red Stain
6 T varathane
1 t cadmium red acrylic paint
1/4 t burnt sienna acrylic paint
Particularly useful on Premo gold clay.

Ochre Stain
6 T varathane
1/2 t cadmium yellow acrylic paint
1/4 t burnt sienna acrylic paint
1/4 t Sunset Gold PearlEx powder
Useful in combination on faux ivory, bone, or wood.

Gold Stain
6 T varathane
1 t metallic gold acrylic paint
1/4 t Brilliant Gold PearlEx powder
1/4 t Aztec Gold PearlEx powder
Best on darker colors, great on black.

Whitewash
2 parts varathane
1 part white acrylic paint
Best mixed and used as needed, as it does not keep well. Use on colors such as green, terra cotta, etc. Gives a whitewash or "pickled" paint effect.

Whitewash looks best on a dark base clay.

T = Tablespoon
t = teaspoon

SAFETY TIPS

When dry sanding or buffing, wear a mask so as not to breathe the dust. When using power tools such as buffing wheels, wear protective eye goggles and a mask for the sake of continued vision and breathing (it's very easy to get a bead caught and flung at you). While baked clay particles are not poisonous, no particulate matter is good for you. Avoid breathing any kind of dust whenever you can. It is irritating, and continued inhalation of any kind of dust can eventually cause an allergic response or worsen existing asthma.

Some artists wear latex gloves while handling raw clay, but people are statistically far more likely to have dermal reactions to the latex and powder in rubber gloves than they are to the clay. If you prefer to wear gloves, try to get ones made of nitrile that don't cause or worsen latex allergies, which is a fast-growing and extremely serious problem in medical and food workers who wear them every day. Keep your exposure to latex at a minimum. Watch out for powdered gloves, which are easier to put on but the powder picks up latex molecules and makes them breathable, and allergic responses are more often provoked by inhalation than by skin contact.

Always wash your hands after working with polymer clay, or with any of the powders, inks, finishes, and pigments you use with it. Remove polymer clay residue from your hands with premoistened wipes or lather your hands with soap and a little water and immediately wipe all of it onto a paper towel. Then wash again with soap and cold water. Even heavy buildups of clay can be easily removed this way. Stains or other finishes that dry on the skin can be gently scrubbed away with warm water and soap and a pumice stone, dish-scrubbing pad, or a rough washcloth.

It's a good idea to regularly use lotion or conditioner on your hands after washing, as dry skin and rough spots make it almost impossible to smooth clay projects with your fingers. You can eliminate a lot of sanding on baked clay by having smooth skin and using your finger to "pet" the raw clay. Your hands are your most important tools, so take care of them. Skin that is dry and cracking leaves marks in raw clay (and it hurts).

Always use a thermometer and check on your items while baking. Try not to forget them in the oven – use a timer if needed. It's also very important to ventilate the baking area. Put a fan in place and open a window or door.

Although polymer clay is tested and certified in the United States as a nontoxic art material, it is always wise to err on the side of caution. Polymer clays should not be used for items that come in direct contact with food or liquids, including perfume oils or lotions (though it is perfectly safe to cover glass bottles that contain these). Nor should they be used on items that will be heated to high temperatures or be in contact with flame. This makes polymer clay unsuitable for dishware or cooking utensils, as well as a very bad idea for smoking pipes, ashtrays, and incense holders that may come in contact with burning embers. It is possible to use polymer clay over candleholders or lamps if the clay is kept away from the heat source. In general, don't cover items meant to get hot or immersed in liquids.

TECHNIQUES: CREATING CANES

"CANES" AND "CANING" ARE TERMS TAKEN FROM

the glassblower's trade. This technique is also known as millefiore (Italian for "thousand flowers"). All sorts of variations in cane design are possible, from the very simple jellyroll spiral to the very complex. Canes can depict geometric shapes, detailed landscapes, snowflakes, flowers, leaves, faces, hair, clothing, butterfly and angel wings, quilt blocks – even signatures! A way to create repetitive patterns, canes are built by compressing clay pieces into certain shapes, then using the colored shapes to build up the desired design in a larger scale than the one seen in the final outcome. After placing all the shapes correctly, like jigsaw puzzle pieces, background clay is added to bring the cane to a shape such as circular, square, or triangular, so it can be reduced. Reducing is done by carefully squeezing, compressing, and gently pulling the clay to move all the components in the desired direction and under equal pressure.

Note: *More information on building and reducing canes can be found in my book,* Create a Polymer Clay Impression.

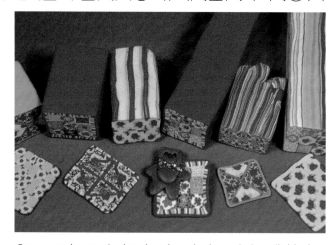

Canes can be manipulated and stacked to mimic quilt blocks.

Jan VanDonkelaar. Seasonal landscapes are meticulously built into these cane slices.

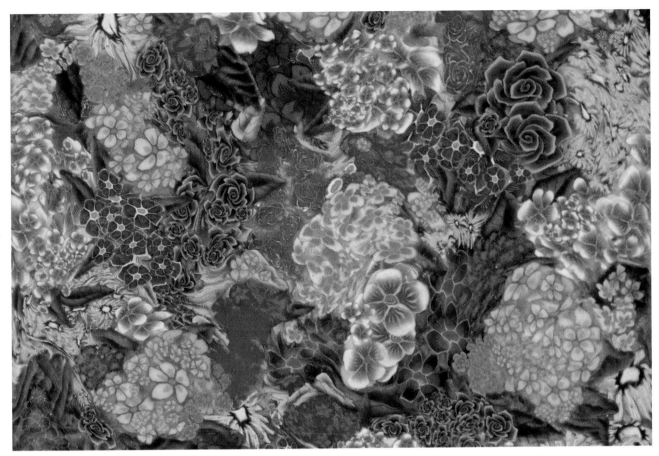

Leigh Ross. These floral canes were applied directly to a ceramic tile. Leigh buffed the finished piece to a high sheen.

Important Tips for Cane Building

1. Use clays of the same consistency. They can all be hard, soft, or in between, but if you use hard and soft clays together, they will not reduce evenly.

2. Choose colors that have high contrast in areas that are significantly reduced – light and dark colors will show better together than two colors in a medium range. Colors mixed with a white clay base will not darken during baking as much as those that have a lot of translucent or pearl in the base. Some colors darken more than others so adding even a little white to the mix helps minimize darkening.

3. Start your canes at least 2" deep or you won't wind up with very much finished cane. The two ends of any cane are always distorted. The amount of distortion depends on the clay consistency and how the cane was built and reduced. The inner section, past the first few inches on either end, usually looks more like the intended image. The end image is often an incomplete part of the intended one and this can be very interesting!

4. Be very careful to tightly pack cane components together so there's no space for shifting. This helps keep distortion to a minimum.

5. Always wrap the outside of a cane with an extra layer of clay. This will protect the image inside during reduction. The outside layer will always reduce faster and more readily because it receives the most pressure, so compensate by adding a wrapping. This clay wrapping will migrate to the cane ends during reduction, which is better than having the outside part of your image moving to the ends. This is especially important with faces. Wrapping also keeps the points on stars nice and sharp since they are at the outside of the image.

6. Allow canes to rest and cool before reduction. This may take a few minutes for small canes or a few hours for large ones.

7. Reduce carefully, and don't rush it. Doing a little at a time will minimize distortion.

Reducing Canes

Stand the cane upright to begin reducing. Use both hands on opposite sides of the cane to press toward the middle, compressing it inward and moving your hands and the cane as you go. Do this until the cane is taller than your hands.

With very large canes, I use an acrylic rod roller or a piece of PVC pipe. I put the bottom of the roller on the work surface, standing upright like the cane, and use my hand to roll it around the cane, pressing toward the center. I use my other hand to hold the cane in place, for resistance. This will smooth out the ridges before they become pronounced.

When the cane pillar has stretched taller than my hands, I lay it on a clean work surface. If it is particularly thick (more than 2" to 3"), I pick it up and throw it down on the table, then roll it a quarter turn so a different part of the surface hits the table. I do this several times to jolt the clay all the way through to the center of the cane, "waking it up" as Z Kripke put it when she showed me this trick. This is a very useful technique if the cane is difficult to reduce due to stiff clay.

Then with all my fingers on the cane, with both hands in the center, I roll the cane back and forth, moving my hands slowly apart and out toward the ends as I go. I give the whole cane a quarter turn (to work a different surface – no part should get too much attention at one time) and roll more. Don't press too hard. If you can see deep finger ridges, you are using too much pressure. Gently push down as you roll, moving toward the ends, but not too quickly.

Flip the cane end to end so that what was the right end becomes the left end. This counteracts the "drift" of the clay, lest it all drift in a continuous clockwise direction (which would result in lopsided faces, etc.). Continue in this way.

Remember to move and flip the cane periodically. It takes time and patience but the faster it goes, the more distortion will occur.

If you feel the clay slipping or moving wrong inside the cane, you may have an air pocket. When this occurs, squeeze the cane gently down on itself, against the work surface, and gently press the outside toward the center. Obvious bubbles can be popped with a pin, and the air pocket carefully removed.

Sarajane Helm. "The Queen of Hearts" features a single cane slice of an intricately made queen image with added borders. Complex parts like the face are made separately, then a portion of it is combined with other detailed canes to build up all sections of the image.

I alternate the rolling reduction technique with a squeeze technique, especially with big canes or canes that are not moving along. To do the squeeze technique, hold the cane in midair with both hands, dangling one end. Place your hands like you are climbing a rope and work your way down the cane, gently squeezing and compressing the cane in on itself. As I work down the length, I let the top part of really big canes rest over my shoulder. Flip the cane end to end, and do it again.

Rolling prevents divots from your fingers and squeezing helps to get things moving. Be careful not to squeeze too much in one place. If the cane gets too long (more than a couple of feet) cut it in half and work each piece separately. Resist the temptation to cut off the ends. Even though the ends are distorted, they protect the rest of the cane. What becomes an end becomes distorted. You can run out of cane if you cut off the ends, so leave them on until you have reduced close to your desired diameter.

Sometimes it helps to use a drawing or photograph, a piece of fabric, or some other image as an inspiration or guide for a design. It's also very satisfying to just play and come up with designs you like. Flowers don't have to be the same as their botanical counterparts! By varying colors, shapes, and direction, even very simple forms can be used to build up beautiful and complex patterns.

Building Canes

When building a cane, the beginning pieces tend to be from a limited number of shapes. Intricate images are built using circles, triangles, rectangles, and lines (made from flat sheets), and most canes can be built using variations of these forms.

Round snakes are long, round, rolled out pieces of clay. These are known as "logs" when they are shorter and fatter (or by those who don't like snakes).

Triangle snakes are made by pinching the top of a round snake while pushing down at the same time to flatten the bottom. Do this down the entire length.

Square snakes are made by using one thumb and forefinger to pinch the sides and the other thumb to flatten the top of the snake against the work surface, making it into a

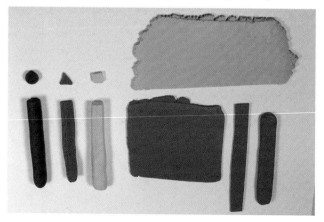

Components of cane building.

long rectangle. Use an acrylic rod or brayer to further level the four sides of the square snake. This makes for very crisp angles in the final design.

Sheets are flat, even layers of clay made by rolling the clay with an acrylic rod, brayer, or pasta machine. Pasta machines produce the most even sheets, with seven to nine predetermined settings that range from 1/8" (#1 on an Atlas machine) to tissue-paper thin (#7 or up to #9 on some machines). Sheets can be used to wrap other components (wrapping a round snake forms a bulls-eye). Sheets can be stacked to make stripes or layered with metallic foils to form "loaves" or stacked canes.

Tongues are clay sheets that are longer than they are wide, and can be thicker (in depth) than a rolled sheet.

Strips are even narrower than tongues and can easily be formed by flattening a snake of clay, using your thumb or a roller to press it flat on the work surface. Run a snake through the pasta machine at the widest setting, then use the noodle cutting attachments for two sizes of strips – thin (spaghetti) and thick (linguini). Just run the clay sheets, which have been rolled to a #1 thickness, through the cutting rollers and out come strips that can be stacked or layered. Strips can also be cut from sheets by hand with a knife.

Cutouts are made using cookie cutters or similar tools. This technique is only suitable with open backed cutters. Make a flattened but still thick lump of conditioned clay (like a burger or hockey puck) around 1" in depth. Powder a cutter lightly on the inside walls. Use it to cut out a shape as desired. Fill in all around the shape using background clay in a strongly contrasting shade. Petit-four cutters are especially good because the cutting walls are several inches deep.

More Notes on Canes

The ends of any reduced cane will be distorted, but this isn't wasted clay. You can often salvage large areas of color and use the clay elsewhere, or mix the clay to form another color. If it's not a color you like, use the clay as a center core and place slices from the canes around it.

You can also use the ends of a cane to make items that coordinate with what you make from the cane itself, as the colors are the ones that form the image, even when the image itself is not clear. Striped and feathered effects can be done easily with the clay from these ends by chopping it up a bit with a knife to distribute the colors. Roll the clay into a fat snake, then twist one end of the snake to roll it while holding the other end still. The more you twist, the tighter the stripes will be. Drag the back of a knife or other tool down the length of the snake, through the stripes, to drag the colors slightly. Repeat at intervals for a feathered effect.

Store canes by wrapping them in plastic wrap such as Saran With Cling. Keep them fresh for long periods by storing them in a box or drawer away from heat and light. Canes that are more than six months old should be rolled a bit before slicing to "wake up" the clay and make it easier to slice.

For easier slicing, hold the blade with both hands and pull your hands slightly apart to create tension in the blade. The blade will go through the cane easier and make cleaner slices. If the blade sticks while slicing, powder it lightly. If the cane is too soft for easy slicing, allow it to sit out for a few hours or a few days to firm it up. Chilling the cane can help in the short term, but if canes are cooled too much, condensation will form and can cause smudges in the final images.

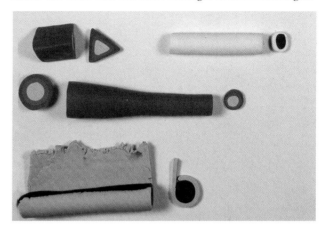

Wrap a snake in a clay sheet to form a bulls-eye.

Stripes can be built with rainbow colors. Slices of stripe canes can be applied around a snake or a bulls-eye. You can build up layers by wrapping sheets around the colored stripe portions.

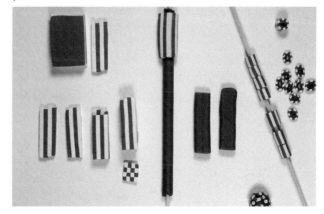

Layers of clay stacked to form stripes. These can be cut and arranged to form checkerboards. Slices from these striped canes can be wrapped around clay to form interesting beads.

Snowflake Canes

Blue and white clay – at least 4 oz. of each for a small cane (more for a larger cane). I used less than 1 lb. of each color to make a large cane.

Making the cane

1. This snowflake was made using stacked sheets of blue and white clay. Roll out a sheet of blue and a sheet of white. Set the pasta roller at the #1 setting or roll by hand to a thickness of around 1/8". Place the white sheet on top of the blue sheet.

2. Smooth out any air bubbles and cut the sheet in half. Stack one on the other so you have blue, white, blue, white. Use a knife to trim this to a rectangle 6" or longer.

3. Cut lengthwise to form three strips, making one a little wider than 1". The next strip should be narrower, and the next one narrower still.

The layers stacked in stair steps.

4. With the widest strip as a base and the blue layer on the bottom, stack the three strips on top of each other so the second strip has equal sized spaces remaining on either side

where the base set shows. Repeat with the third narrowest strip. It should be like stair steps on both sides.

Pack with background and bring to square.

5. Cut strips of blue from another #1 (1/8" thick) sheet to lay down on either side to fill in the spaces. Place the narrower strips on the bottom

Cut the resulting rectangle in half.

layers and add the progressively wider ones to fill in the empty parts to form a rectangle rather than a triangle. Put a layer of blue across the entire top. This is now a striped stack.

6. Cut this rectangle in half down through the center of the stripes so it looks like two sets of white stairs and a blue background.

7. Lay the cut face of one section down on a #1 (1/8" thick) tongue of white clay, then trim the white clay to fit. Carefully place the other blue/white section so the white stripes are evenly matched from one side to the other. This forms the first section of the snowflake cane.

8. To shape the section for the next step, pinch the entire cane along the top and sides to shape the cane into a triangle. The design should look a little like a white tree.

Pinch the cane along the top and sides to form a triangle.

9. Hold the point end of the tri-angle and push the base sides up toward the point so the cane becomes a diamond shape. Do this along the entire length of the cane.

10. Trim the ends of the cane and cut it into six equal sections.

11. Use a white clay snake as a center. Make this central snake as large as it needs to be to fit the cut sections around it neatly, with the wider base portions facing the center. Pay attention to the placement – it is very easy to accidentally put one in upside down, as you can see I did (mistakes can be visually acceptable in the final smaller scale). Use blue triangle snakes to fill in as needed at the center between sections and at the outside layer (you will need bigger triangle snakes for this).

Reduce the cane, stack, and reduce again.

12. Let the cane rest for at least a half an hour, then reduce it.

13. Cut a section of the cane into two equal lengths, then cut one of them down the length of the cane to form half-circle canes. Cut those in half to form quarters. Arrange these quarter sections, points out, spaced evenly around the other snowflake cane section to start to form a square cane. Fill in the empty divots between the quarters with blue clay, then reduce the square cane to compact it firmly and take the scale down further (which helps hide my mistake in the upside down section).

14. Cut the square cane into four equal sections and stack the sections with two side by side and two on top. Use careful placement to join the quarter sections (corners) into as clean an image as possible, but don't worry about a little distortion (all snowflakes are different, after all). Reduce very slightly to firmly press everything together and form a tidy square cane. The repeat pattern that is formed in this way is very much like fabric designs.

Carol L. Simmons developed a very geometrically precise technique for making snowflake canes that is more complex and results in fabulously detailed canes. Here are some results of that technique.

A Simpler Snowflake

This snowflake is a bit simpler to make.

You will need

Blue and white clay – at least 4 oz. of each for a small cane (more for a larger cane)

Making the cane

1. For an easier snowflake cane, start the cane with only one layer of blue and white stripes instead of two, and keep the resulting cane segment as a triangle, not pushing the base up to form a diamond.

The stair step stripes.

2. Place the triangle segments around a small white snake center with the points of the triangle facing the center and the base on the outside. Pack with blue between the sections if needed and reduce.

3. Wrap the entire cane in a layer of blue clay to help preserve the image when reducing.

A snowflake cane of white and translucent, and a slice stretched over a blue background.

Other variations include using a more complex center instead of a single white snake. The snowflake canes shown above were made using white and translucent for the background instead of blue. When a thin slice of that cane is placed on a piece of blue clay and stretched a bit, the background color shows through. In this way, you can vary the background color while using a single translucent/white cane.

A variety of translucent and white lace canes.

By using translucent and white clays to form a cane, you can achieve a very lacy, airy effect. When baked, slices of these canes turn a beige to ochre color, which can be pleasing in itself, or very thin slices of the canes can be used over any colored base and the color will show through the translucent areas. If enough care is taken to slice very thinly, and the baked piece is sanded and buffed, the translucent becomes glassy and almost completely transparent.

To avoid or reduce darkening the translucent clays, be very careful to use the correct temperature – usually slightly lower than other clays – and also not to bake it too long. Follow the package directions for the brand of translucent clay you're using. I have found that avoiding contact with the baking surface also helps keep the translucent from browning, so I bake translucent pieces in a nest of fiberfill polyester batting or stuffing, or on a sheet of cardstock placed on top of a few wads of fiberfill, which raises it up from the pan's surface.

The simple slices in the photo show jellyroll, bulls-eye, and striped canes made with Premo translucent and white clays. When combined, these shapes can be made to look much like lace or broderie anglais, which is a white-on-white embroidery technique used in making eyelet lace fabric. Slices of the lace canes can be used to decorate clothing on polymer clay dolls and figures or as wonderful airy backgrounds for floral canes (see the Spring Flowers Boxed Set, page 54).

For a great faux ivory/bone effect, stack and roll sheets of white and translucent through a pasta machine at the setting between #3 and #6 or by hand to a thickness of between 1/16" and 1/32". Layer the sheets until you have a stack a little over 1/4" thick and put it through the pasta roller again at a #1 or #2 setting or roll by hand to a thickness of around 1/8". This compresses the stripes. Cut equal sized pieces and stack them on top of each other. Press lightly to meld them together and to reduce the new striped cane further if desired. You can make great faux wood grain this way as well, and also pinstripes when using other colors.

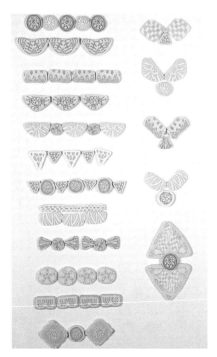

Combine canes to increase the resemblance to lace with intricate repetitions.

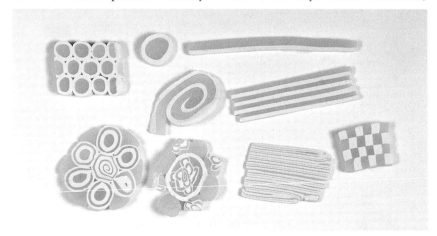

Simple shapes in canes of translucent and white, which combine to build lacy designs.

Slices can be placed on a sheet of white or pearl white clay and rolled with a pasta roller until they all meld together, but the chance of picking up a fleck of color is very high when putting anything with translucent through the roller (and it's invariably a turquoise blotch or a red spot, right on the dainty parts!). I usually roll these sheets out with an acrylic rod or cover the surface of the clay with a stretched-flat piece of Saran Wrap before putting it through the pasta machine (any wrinkles will be pressed into the clay, so try to avoid them). The resulting patterned sheet can be baked and used flat, or you can cut shapes from the raw sheets.

The glued mosaic of cane slices pictured was made by Leigh Ross. I scanned the mosaic and used the scan to make lovely greeting cards. Individual slices bake darker than ones on a sheet of backing clay.

Translucent clays can also be used as background fill in other canes, especially on the outer edges. Images can be overlapped or butted together in wonderful ways. Leigh's "Millennium Garden" (see page 97) floral images are done in this manner, as are some of the floral canes shown next.

Leigh Ross. Baked slices of lace canes.

FLORAL CANES

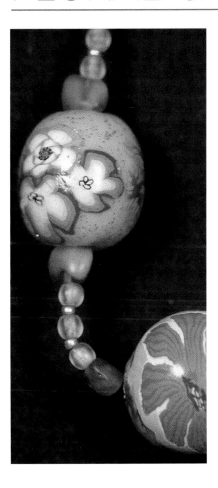

To make a floral cane, you usually need a center, petals, and perhaps a leaf or two. Centers can be a simple snake or bulls-eye, or a grouping of them. Spirals (jellyrolls) make great centers for roses. Petals can be fat and rounded, long and thin, or in single rows or layers. You can make petals a solid color or shade them horizontally or vertically.

To create canes of flowers from my garden, I scanned fresh-picked blossoms and used the printouts for inspiration and reference.

When making these floral canes, remember that mathematical precision is not a requirement. Pasta roller settings are given in these instructions as a general guide, but if your pasta machine settings are different widths than mine, of if you don't use a machine, it's not critical. What is important is consistency – try to use the same thickness sheet as a wrap for the entirety of the petal section. Don't use a sheet that is 1/16" in some places and 1" thick in others.

In general terms, the widest (#1) setting on an Atlas pasta roller is twice as thick as the #3 setting, which is twice as thick as the #6 setting. With a Pasta Queen, numbers are reversed so that a #7 is the widest and sheets from it are about twice as thick as a #5, which is about twice as thick as a #2. Each machine varies slightly over time as well, so don't get too caught up in the arithmetic. It is more important that the clay pieces stay relative to each other. The numbers aren't as important as that the outline is thinner than the piece it surrounds, and so on.

When reduced, sheets of the thinnest settings are as good as invisible, so I rarely go beyond a #5 setting, which is 1/24" thick before reduction of the cane. All cane-making directions in this book use Atlas machine settings for reference, but it is quite possible to make canes without using a roller. I did it that way for years.

You will need

1 oz. yellow clay

2 oz. light pink clay (mix of white and reds and pinks)

2 oz. medium pink (mix light pink with a little black or green to get a slightly darker shade)

1 oz. darker pink clay

3 oz. background green clay (I mixed Premo Sap Green with ecru and white)

1 oz. white clay

Making the complex center

1. Roll the yellow into a pencil sized snake and trim to 4" long.

2. Roll out some of the dark pink through a pasta roller at the #3 setting or by hand to a thickness of around 1/16". Wrap this around the yellow to form a bulls-eye. Reduce to a diameter of 1/4". Cut into 2" pieces. (I had seven pieces, but the number is not important.)

3. Bundle the 2" pieces together to form the complex center and trim again to 2" in length.

4. Mix the cut off ends with an equal amount of the darker pink and blend completely. Roll this mixture out to form very small snakes. Cut as many as you can to the 2" length. These don't have to be even in width, variance is okay here.

5. Place these around the outside perimeter of the center, leaving some spaces.

6. Roll out a similar small diameter snake of the dark pink clay and fill in the spaces. Surround the entire center.

7. Roll out a similar snake of the medium pink and lay several sections on top of the other pink snakes. Do the same with the lightest pink clay. Compress lightly.

8. Reduce this to a cane that is 1/2" in diameter.

9. Trim off the ends and cut a section 2" to 3" long. You should have enough of this complex center to make two or three different floral canes.

10. Wrap the remaining cane length in Saran Wrap to store it. It is such a small part that you will be able use sections in very different flowers effectively (see "Wild Rose Cane," page 37).

Adding vertical shading to the petals

1. Roll out all the light pink clay into a thick snake about as wide as your thumb. Flatten the snake with your thumb or a roller to form a strip approximately 1" wide and several inches long.

2. Do the same with the medium pink clay and stack the medium pink strip on top of the light pink. Compress, flatten, and form into a tongue of clay at least 12" long and 1-1/2" wide. Cut the tongue into sections and stack them in three or four layers to get the striped effect.

3. Reduce the stack to 12" in length again.

4. Turn the stack so the stripes along the side are visible on top. Roll out small white snakes and place them in the grooves between the layers. Do this on one side only – this will be the top of the petal and will make a slightly ruffled petal edge rather than a smooth one.

5. Roll white clay through a pasta roller at the #4 setting or by hand to a thickness of less than 1/16". Wrap this sheet around the petal stack. Cover half of the top and bottom of the stack and one side with white snakes. Don't cover the other side. It's easiest to lay the white on the work surface and place the stack on it so the white snakes at the petal top are laid down on and following the midline of the white strip. Fold the rest up onto the petal stack, making sure this U of clay doesn't wrap around the entire stack and that some pink and white shows down the sides and bottom of the petal piece.

6. Roll to reduce enough to firmly affix the white sheet. Use a needle to pop air bubbles if necessary. Reduce a bit more, making sure it doesn't get too thin, then pinch the uncovered side of the stack to form the inside point of the petals.

7. Round the covered side slightly by pinching it to form a petal shape (a somewhat rounded triangle or teardrop).

8. Reduce and cut into eight sections using the center section of the flower to measure.

9. With the pointed (uncovered with white) section in, arrange the petal sections around the center section. The petals should all touch the center area, with spaces (divots) left between them on the outside near the top of the petals.

Adding the green background

1. Roll out half of the light green clay into a snake as thick as your index finger. Pinch and flatten it to form a triangle snake.

2. Cut the snake to fit the length of your cane and fit the pointed part between the petal sections to fill in the divots. Press in to fill – there should be enough that parts of this triangle shape go over the top to help protect the roundness of the petals.

3. Check the placement of all pieces by looking at the top and bottom of the cane where the pattern shows, then compress the whole cane toward the center. The outer sides of the cane column should now show a pattern of thin white and wider green stripes. Use green strips of flattened clay to cover all the exposed white.

4. Allow the cane to rest for 20 minutes, then carefully reduce it to the desired diameter. I often stop at 1" or slightly larger (it can be reduced more later).

5. Cut off the ends until you come to a relatively undistorted image.

6. Cut into four sections and wrap one section of the cane for later use at this size. Reduce one of the sections to half the diameter, wrap, and set aside. Use two of the sections to build a square cane (see Repeating Patterns, page 38).

Variations

A horizontally shaded purple flower.

Slight changes to the cosmos flower can result in a whole garden full of flowers. Use different colors for the petals or the centers. Choose

Another variation with vertical shaded petals and several sections of the center cane, combined.

thicker or thinner stripes in the petals – which themselves can be made fatter or thinner, longer or shorter, fewer or in more profusion. The wide variety in Mother Nature's garden means there's lots of room for play with your clay.

Building the blue flower.

I made the blue flower shown with a center of bulls-eye snakes in yellow and blue around a darker yellow center snake. I made the petals with three stripes in the beginning stack – dark blue, white, and light blue. I put dark blue on the bottom of the stack and laid an additional piece of dark blue on top of the final stack before reducing it. I used small triangle snakes of translucent Premo clay for the background.

When the cane is reduced, thin slices of it can be applied over any background clay, and the translucent background will almost disappear (with careful smoothing and burnishing). With patient sanding and buffing, a tremendous sheen can be achieved.

Colors mixed in a pearl clay base darken when baked, which can produce subtle shades.

The photo above shows a version of the cosmos flower made with pearl clays, colors mixed with pearl red and pearl white. Colors with a pearl base darken far more than matte clays.

A compound bulls-eye center for the daisy.

The daisy petal is made of long thin strips of beige and ivory.

Try vertical shaded petals with a single bulls-eye center like the daisy shown, or shorter petals with another longer row outside. This requires making much more of the petal cane to begin with, but is well worth the effort.

You can use floral canes to make floral beaded necklaces or earrings. A very simple way to make disc beads is to cut a cane into segments thick enough to be pierced with a needle. This is usually between 1/4" and 3/8". With a little practice you will get very efficient at poking through the middle. It helps to twist the needle around as you push through, so that it acts more like a drill. Beads can also be baked first and drilled after baking.

Marigold Cane

You will need

2 oz. red clay
2 oz. orange clay
2 oz. yellow clay
2 oz. translucent clay
4" of flower center cane (from cosmos or other flower)

Making the cane

1. Mix half the yellow clay with a little orange so you have a dark yellow for petals and a light yellow for the outline. Make thick snakes of the red, orange, and dark yellow clays, and flatten them to 1" wide and several inches long, just as with the cosmos flower cane. Cut and place these on top of each other to form a striped stack of yellow, red, yellow, orange, yellow, red. Don't use a pasta machine here; you want the stripes to have subtle variations in width.

2. Compress, flatten, and form the layers into a stack of clay at least 12" long and close to 1" wide.

3. Turn the stack so the stripes along the side are visible on top. Roll out thin snakes of dark yellow and add them in the divots between the red orange and dark yellow stripes to make the ruffled edges. Repeat on the opposite side and on both sides of the striped stack (the cosmos cane only does this to one side). For visible petal edges, roll a thin sheet of red clay (#5 or 1/24"), cut it to fit, and lay it over the top of the snakes added to form the ruffled edges of the petal both at the top and bottom of the stack. You can cover the sides as well if you wish (I didn't in this example). Then cover the entire stripe stack with a #4 (1/20") sheet of light yellow. If you are doing yellow petals, use red here for contrast.

4. Reduce as for the cosmos petal, and place it on the work surface so the stripes are stacked horizontally. Use a knife to cut down the center of the cane along the full length. This gives you two petal canes, with petals half as tall. Each cane has one ruffled end and one cut end. Squeeze the sides of each to narrow the bottoms of the cane, but don't bring to a real point. Cut to make between 20 and 24 equal length pieces.

5. Build a flower center. You can use a simple snake, bulls-eyes, or get more complex by building a center with six 1" pieces of the cosmos center. (There was a lot of it left over and it's easy to use in other flowers.) Place the center pieces together around a snake of red, press together, and reduce to make a complex center for the marigold. It should no longer look like the cosmos center. It should now show multiple tiny yellow and red specks, much as real marigolds do. Cut a section the same length as your petal pieces and place six of the petals around the center. Place another layer of petals on top of this one, staggering them so a new petal section starts in the middle of a petal on the layer below. Add the rest of the petal sections. This may require a third row with fewer petal sections, so arrange them pleasingly around the circumference with space in between as needed.

6. Add snakes of translucent clay between the final row of petals to make the cane circular again. Allow it to rest for 20 minutes, then reduce to the desired size.

Wild Rose Cane

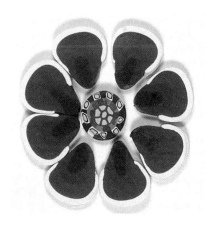

This flower has horizontally shaded and very rounded petals. An easy way to build the petals is to form a striped stack in gradated colors – from light to dark – then bend that stack halfway around a snake of the last shade in the progression. Point the other end or the exposed snake to form a teardrop-shaped petal. This flower uses both Premo red clays – Alizarin Crimson (deep bluish red) and Cadmium Red (flame red). Together they make rich Christmas red.

You will need

2 oz. crimson
2 oz. cadmium red
2 oz translucent
2 oz. white
3" piece cosmos flower center
1 oz. green (optional)

Horizontal shading for the wild rose petal, and the section of cosmos center.

Making the cane

1. Roll thick snakes and flatten them as for the cosmos and marigold petals.

2. Stack the flattened strips of clay, starting with crimson, followed by a mix of crimson and cadmium, then one with more cadmium red, and so on.

3. Bend the stack halfway around a thick snake (about as wide as your finger) of crimson, making sure to place the crimson face of the stack against the snake. Point the other end or the exposed snake to form a teardrop-shaped petal.

4. Wrap the top rounded section of the cane in a #5 sheet (1/24") of white for a crisp outline against the background. This will make the dark petals show up against a dark or medium background and will keep the red petals from bleeding or smearing into other areas. As with the cosmos flower petal, don't cover the entire petal – stop about halfway down the sides of the teardrop.

5. To make the center, start with a section of the center used for the cosmos. Make yellow snakes wrapped in black, then in white. Add these small bulls-eye snakes around the center. Between each bulls-eye snake on the outside of the center, add a very small triangle snake of crimson (the innermost petal color). This will make the yellow bulls-eye pieces appear to be rising up from the dark red portion of the petals in the final cane.

6. Cut the petal cane into seven or eight sections. Arrange the petals around the center. I cut eight, but they didn't fit snuggly around the center, so I used seven of the sections to form the wild rose cane and saved one piece to make a bud cane. This is a great way to use a leftover.

7. Roll triangular translucent snakes and use them to fill the divots between each petal. Wrap the entire cane with a thin (#5 or 1/24") layer of translucent to help keep the roundness of the petals. Reduce the wild rose cane to the desired size.

To make a bud using a petal section, lay two thin strips of green clay so one is on each side of the bottom point of the petal. They should meet so no petal point is exposed. (You can use one piece and bend it if you prefer.) This green becomes the calyx of the flower, which is not as visible on full-blown versions of flowers shown face-on, but does show on buds. Reduce this bud cane as desired.

Roll out a small strip of clay and use it to cover a wooden bead.

1. To make beads, wrap a small strip of background clay around a wooden bead or a round piece of clay. Pull very slightly as you wrap and cut off excess clay so the clay ends meet but don't overlap. Leave the bead hole ends slightly exposed, as the clay will stretch to cover and you don't want too much excess.

2. Roll the clay-covered bead in your palms to smooth it. If the bead holes become covered, poke them with a stick or bead reamer to keep them open.

3. Cut thin slices of canes and place them on the clay background.

4. Roll again in your hands to meld the slices to the background. Poke the holes again on each end if needed to make them neat.

5. Slide the bead on a bamboo skewer for baking. You can fit several at a time on a skewer, but don't allow them to touch each other. Leave the ends of the skewer empty and suspend the skewer between the sides of a baking pan to keep the beads from touching the pan itself. The skewer also makes beads easier to coat with finishes later. I usually fill an entire pan before baking.

6. Bake according to package directions.

Yellow Rose Variation

Build up layers going from dark to light, and wrap the stack entirely around a snake of the lightest color.

For this yellow rose, the shaded petals are fatter than for the wild rose. Start with a striped stack that goes from light to dark. Wrap the striped stack completely around a snake of clay made with the lightest color to make a multiple layered bulls-eye.

Slice this down the entire length of the cane to form two half-circle canes. Use these half-circles to form the petals around the center used in the wild rose cane. Add one or two

Slice this cane lengthwise down through the center to form two long half-circle canes. Use pieces as petals to build the yellow rose cane.

rows of petals as desired. Add triangular translucent snakes in the divots between petals. Reduce to the desired size.

Repeating Patterns

Use sections to build a square cane.

Squared canes that look like repeating fabric designs can be made using two equal sections of round canes.

1. Start with two equal sections of your original cane. Add more clay, either the same background used in the cane or a totally different color that coordinates with the colors in the cane.

2. Slice down the length of one cane section, making two half-circle canes. Place both flat side down and

again cut down the length of the middle of each, making a total of four quarter wedges.

3. Apply each quarter section to the remaining round length of cane, with the points of the quarter sections facing out. These become the corners of the square cane. There may be a small empty space between each quarter section as you space them evenly around the round length. If so, fill the spaces with small (sized to fit the space) snakes of the correct length made of the other clay.

4. Gently squeeze the resulting square cane to slightly compress it. The cane can be reduced by carefully compressing the cane inward, working up and down the length with even pressure of your fingers. Or use

an acrylic rod, brayer, or PVC roller down the length of each side of the cane, pressing gently into the work surface.

5. The square cane may be further changed by cutting and stacking pieces of equal length. This gives a repeat pattern effect where the corners meet and recombine the original flower design. You can continue to reduce, cut, and recombine pieces of square cane, or use them as they are.

Multiple square canes can be stacked to make repeat designs.

Simple Leaf Canes

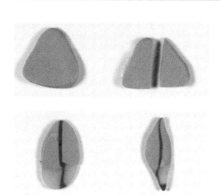

A simple leaf.

You will need

2 oz. green clay
1 oz. dark green clay
2 oz. translucent clay

Making the leaf cane

1. Roll a green snake about as thick as your finger and pinch it to a point. Roll it to about 12" long.

2. Slice the triangle down the

length from the point to the base and add a thin strip of clay cut from a #1 sheet of dark green between the two sections for the vein. Let the end of the dark green strip extend about 1/8" past the wider section bottom of the cut triangle snake.

3. Add small snakes of translucent on either side of this extended bit to hold it in place. Pinch and reduce slightly. An alternative is to make a dark leaf with a light vein.

Compound Leaf Canes

Put simple leaf canes together to make a compound leaf.

You will need

simple leaf cane
1 oz. translucent clay
small amount of dark green clay used in simple leaf

Making the cane

1. To make it a compound leaf, build a simple leaf cane and cut it into five equal lengths.

2. Cut a strip of dark green clay about 1" wide and as long as the five leaf cane sections. Place one cut section at the side of the darker green strip, butting it so the extended vein of the leaf meets the green strip.

3. Lay two other leaf sections on top of the strip as shown.

4. Fill in the areas between the leaf parts with small triangles of translucent.

5. Flip the whole thing over and add the other two sections. Fill as before with the translucent for the background.

6. Reduce the cane and slightly pinch the top to create a point.

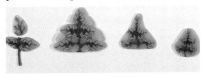

A complex fern leaf.

To make very complex leaves, such as ferns, cut the compound leaf cane into five sections and use it to build the fern leaf as you did the compound leaf, laying the pieces along a strip of green.

Cosmo Leaf Cane

Cosmo leaf cane. This leaf has no center vein, and the stripes look like individual fronds when reduced.

You will need

2 oz. light green clay (I mixed Premo Sap Green, white, and gold)
1 oz. dark green clay
1 oz. white clay

Making the leaf cane

1. Roll out all the dark green clay into a snake about as thick as your finger. Flatten the snake with your thumb to at least 1/2" wide and 12" long.

2. Do the same with the white and stack the white snake on top of the green snake. Compress, flatten, and roll out into a tongue of clay at least 12" long and 3/4" wide. The depth of the tongue should be around 1/4" or larger.

3. Cut this tongue into three sections. Stack and reduce to 12" again, making a striped stack.

4. Press down along one side of the stack to form a point. Reduce into a triangular cane, pulling and pinching gently along the length of the cane.

5. Cut into five sections. Place one section as the top of the leaf, with the pointed part down. Place another section to the left and slightly down, and another on the right in the same way. Add two more, bringing the sections together at the bottom.

6. Roll out a snake of light green background clay and flatten it slightly to form a tongue of clay about 1/4" thick. Cut sections of this tongue and lay them on top of the leaf sections where they protrude at the sides.

7. Flatten one strip further and lay it over the top part of the leaf.

8. Roll out the remaining light green and use it to wrap the leaf cane and fill it in to a triangular cane as shown.

9. Reduce.

FACE CANES

Face canes.

Faces are the hardest and most persnickety of all canes to build and reduce because the elements must be precisely placed. (It won't do to have the eyes on top of or under the nose!) I find it helps to start with a drawing or sketch to aid in placement of the sections when building face canes.

Add small amounts of white to flesh toned clays to eliminate the darkening that naturally occurs while baking. Because the clay is then a custom mix, always make more than you think you will need. It is much harder to match a mix later unless you have kept track of the proportions.

Tips for face canes

1. Start by building one eye and one cheek. When reduced, these can be cut in half to make two of each. When making the eyes, place triangles of white clay on either side of the iris (don't wrap white all around the iris or you'll get a "pop" eye).

2. Wrap a layer of skin tone clay around the cheek to keep it rounded. Otherwise, when compressing the facial elements together you will end up with pointy parts where the cheek color distorts.

3. For an outlined look, wrap a thin sheet (#5 or 1/24") of black clay

around the eyes, nose, and mouth. This is most effective with adult faces. For a softer, more childlike look, wrap these elements with brown clay.

4. The placement of the cane elements is very important. Think of the face as a circle and imagine two lines dividing it in half, both vertically and horizontally. Place the eyes in the top half of the face, slightly above the horizontal line, with approximately an eye's worth of space between them. This space is where the nose goes. The mouth is approximately the size of an eye. The distance from the bottom of the nose to the top of the mouth is about the same as the vertical measurement of the eye. The cheeks are only slightly larger than the eye, but the cheeks are round and the eyes are more almond-shaped (even in occidental faces, the eyes are not really round because of the lids). Place the cheeks under the eyes, with an eye's worth of space between the bottom of the eye and the top of the cheek. Place the cheeks slightly to the outside, not directly under the eyes.

5. There is a lot of packing of the flesh areas to be done (you will need more flesh clay than you think). It is vital to wrap the assembled face cane in a thick outer layer of flesh clay. When reduced, the outer parts of the cane flow to the ends and are no longer part of the finished design. If the eyes and cheeks are left at the outside edges with no protection, they will reduce away to almost nothing, while the nose, protected at the center of the cane, becomes huge. I now know to wrap a lot of flesh color around face canes before reduction. When reduction is well along, I often wrap a brown or black layer on the outside of the cane to give each slice a definite line of demarcation at the chin area. The rest of this line is usually covered by hair canes.

Note: *I usually make face canes without the hair. After the face cane is*

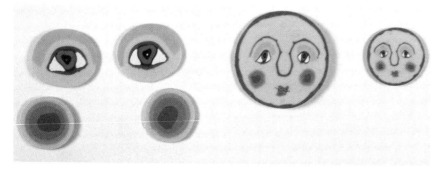

The placement of eyes and cheeks of a face cane are shown on the left, and the finished face cane is shown on the right.

reduced, you can cut it in several sections and add hair to them if desired or use slices individually and add hair to those. This gives you much greater range in design.

6. After the face cane is reduced, don't despair if it isn't quite as you planned or if it's crooked. The final look can be changed significantly by reshaping the cane or manipulating the individual slices. If an eye or mouth is askew, cut a slice (not too thin, you need enough clay to work with without tearing) and place your index finger and thumb on the top and underside in the place you want to move, and gently tweak it into place. If an eye or mouth is too small, place a tiny amount of clay underneath to pad the slice in the area you wish to enlarge, and spread the image gently out as you flatten the area. If something looks too large, reduce the feature slightly by carefully pushing the parts of it in on itself. (For example, a honker nose can be reduced by pushing both sides of the nose toward the middle.) Don't use too much pressure or the elements will smear. These techniques take a little bit of practice but you will be amazed by the powers of "plastic surgery!"

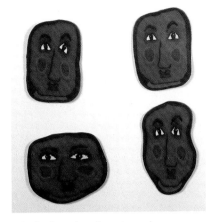

Manipulate the slices to make individual faces.

Making a Face Cane

You will need

4 oz. black clay (or 1 lb. if you are doing a final wrap in black)
2 lb. flesh clay
4 oz. white clay
2 oz. eye color clay (brown, blue, green, etc.)
2 oz. cheek color clay

Face canes start out large, in order to build in detail. They are also made in several sections – eyes, cheeks, nose, mouth – then packed in place with background flesh color. This version was made with around 2-1/2 lb. of clay. You can make smaller or larger versions as desired. You will have some extra of the various segments. I used some of the leftover lip to make a simple rose cane. The ends from the final face cane can be mixed to make another color or used as backing for appliquéd pins or centers of beads. It is better to have too much of a cane section than not enough.

In this version, I used skin tone mix made from 1 lb. of ecru, 1 lb. of base (an uncolored clay that makes the final tone a bit less matte), and 2 oz. of white. Mixing some white with the skin tone helps keep it from darkening while baking.

Eyes

The beginning bulls-eye.

1. Roll out a 1/8" wide by 2" long snake of white clay for the highlight of the eye. Roll out a black snake 2" long and as thick as your finger. Flatten the black snake with your thumb, making it wider, not longer.

Place the white snake down the center of the black and roll the black around it. Reduce until it measures 4" long.

2. Roll out 1 oz. of the eye color (I used burnt sienna) and wrap the black snake in it. Trim the ends until you see the white highlight as well as the black pupil. Reduce to 6".

Add white triangles on each side.

3. Roll out a white snake 1/2" wide by 12" long. Pinch the top and flatten it on the work surface to shape it into a triangle snake. Cut two 6" pieces, and place them on either side of the eye cane. Press lightly to firmly adhere the triangles to the eye.

4. Wrap the entire thing with a #5 (1/24") sheet of black clay (pop any trapped air bubbles).

5. Roll out a sheet of #1 (1/8") flesh clay and wrap it around the eye. Trim the ends to neaten them.

6. Mix the trimmings (it should have a little black and a little eye color) with 2 oz. of the flesh color to make a shadow color. Roll this out to a #1 tongue, and double it by folding it on itself. Lay this down on top of the eye.

Wrap with flesh color clay.

7. Roll out another #1 layer of flesh color and wrap the entire eye. Reduce slightly to the desired size and cut two 4" sections to make two eyes. Set aside.

Cheeks

Note: *The color you choose for the cheeks will affect the amount you use in the blending process. Deep colors like the crimson I use here require a much smaller amount to blend lovely pinks.*

1. Mix 1/2 oz. red with 2 oz. flesh to make a dark pink. Cut off 1/4 of that mixture, and mix it with 2 oz. of flesh to make a medium pink.

2. Roll out a dark pink snake 6" long by 3/4" diameter, or slightly larger.

3. Roll out the medium pink to a #1 sheet and wrap it around the dark pink. Cut off the excess medium pink.

The three-layer cheek.

4. Add the remaining medium pink to 2 oz. of flesh to make a light pink. Roll this into a flat sheet and wrap it around the medium pink.

5. Reduce this three-layer cheek bulls-eye to 12" in length.

6. Trim the ends and cut a 7" piece for the cheeks. Set aside the remaining 5" piece (it will be used for the lips).

7. Wrap the 7" cheek piece with a #1 layer of flesh color. Reduce to about 1" diameter.

8. Cut two sections 4" long. Put these aside with the eyes.

Lips

1. For the lips, use the remaining 5" section of the pink bulls-eye cane. Roll to reduce it to 1/2" diameter.

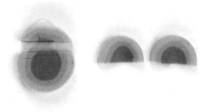

Use the bottom section for the lips.

2. Cut a 4" section. Use a blade to shave off the top, moving down the length of the cane. Cut deep enough to just expose the dark pink – not quite halfway. The bottom part of the circle will be the lower lip.

3. Reduce the remaining pink bulls-eye to about 3/8" diameter. Shave the top layer from this as well and cut it into two 4" pieces. The bottom of the cut circle will be used as the upper lips.

4. Mix the cut-off tops with an equal amount of crimson. Roll out a #3 (1/16") strip 1" wide and 4" long. This is the "smile" part of the lips.

Add the two upper lips and one lower lip to the "smile" strip.

5. Place the flat shaved section of the lower lip on top of this strip, running down the center with equal amounts of the strip showing on either side. Flip this over and add the two upper lip sections. There will be a space between the two upper lip pieces even though they butt right up to each other. Fill the space with a small triangle snake of flesh.

6. Flip it over again and slightly bend the smile line up around the outside edges of the upper lip sections to give it a little curve. Add small triangle snakes on either side of the lower lip.

7. Wrap the entire lip section in a #1 (1/8") sheet of flesh clay. Reduce to around 3/4" diameter (more or less, depending on the desired size) and cut a 4" section. Place this aside with the cheeks and eyes.

Nose

1. Mix 4 oz. flesh with 1/2 oz. white to make a slightly lighter skin shade (adjust the amount of white as desired).

2. Roll out a #1 sheet of this light skin color and cut out a 4" by 4-1/2" rectangle.

3. Roll out and cut a sheet of flesh the same size and place it on top of the light piece.

4. Roll out a #6 (1/32") sheet of black and place it on top of the flesh layer. Pop any air bubbles.

5. Roll out another layer of flesh to a #1 (1/8") thickness and cut another rectangle the same size. Stack this on top of the black layer. You should now have a striped stack that measures 4" by 4-1/2" and is layered as follows: light skin, flesh, black, flesh.

6. Roll out a snake of the remaining light skin clay about as wide as your finger (1/2" or slightly larger) and flatten it slightly. Cut to 4" in length. Place the striped nose stack in front of you with the longer part running from side to side and the light skin layer on top.

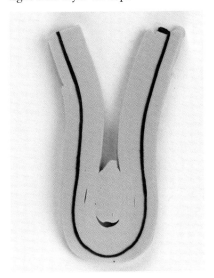

Wrap the striped stack around the snake.

7. Place the light skin snake on top of the stack, down the center, so it runs from front to back and there is about 2" of the striped stack showing on the right and left of the snake. This snake becomes the ball or tip of the nose. Fold the striped stack up and around on either side of the snake to form a U shape.

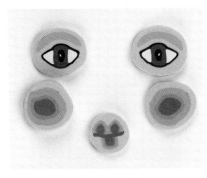

Check the relative size of the components as well as the placement.

8. Place the eyes on either side of the nose piece. Bring the top of each side of the nose stack up and out to form eyebrows, carefully smoothing the brows over the eyes. Pinch the

nose section as needed to form it as you like, but try to keep the bottom slightly rounded.

Form eyebrows around the eyes.

Note: When putting the eye, cheek, and lip components together, flip the entire thing over periodically to check that it is correct on both sides and tweak as needed to align.

9. Fill the space in the middle top of the nose with a large flesh triangle snake. Fill the two smaller triangle spaces between the inside bottom of the eyes and the nose with smaller flesh triangle snakes as well.

10. Place the cheeks below the eyes and slightly to the outside. Fill in all the spaces between the cheeks and nose with flesh snakes.

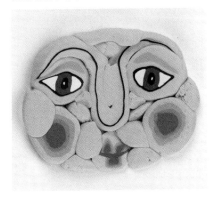

The cut-off end of this face cane shows the placement of all pieces held in place by the flesh background. Some of the pieces have already moved a bit in compressing the cane. The face is shown before the final wrap of flesh clay.

11. Place the lips directly below the nose. Fill in all spaces with more flesh snakes. This should bring you to a rounded shape for the face. Compress the outside edges slightly

toward the center to make sure any air pockets are removed.

12. You should still have almost half of the original skin tone. (If not, make more until you have around a pound of it.) Use this to wrap the outside of the entire face cane. Many people forget this step, then wonder why the facial features are not the right proportions after reduction. You must wrap a lot because much of it will move to the ends during the reduction process. It's better to lose the fleshy outsides than the eyes and mouth!

13. Press the sides of the cane in toward the center to make sure all parts adhere well to each other. At this point, the cane measures 3-1/2" across by 5" tall.

Reduce very carefully to avoid unwanted distortion.

14. Allow the cane to rest for several hours before reduction. Reduce by pressing the sides toward the center and working up and down the cane with your hands. It will be tough going at first, but don't rush it. Rest the clay and your hands every once in a while. As the clay reduces in diameter, it grows in length. When it gets long enough, hold it like a rope in front of you and work up and down the length, squeezing but not twisting. Gravity, and the cane's own weight will start to help with the reduction. If it begins to go too fast, stop and allow the cane to cool a bit. Eventually you will need to cut the cane in half to work on it more easily. You can also trim the outer ends until you get to the part with a good clear face. This will take several inches on either end, but don't despair, this is one reason to make them big in the first place. Also, this end clay can always be used as a backing or as a core in beads, so it doesn't go to waste.

15. Keep reducing until the cane is 1" to 2" in diameter. You can always reduce it more later for smaller faces. Wrap the face with more skin color if you think it needs it or wrap it with a #5 layer of black if you want a sharp outline to mark the chin area and so on.

16. Cut the cane into segments and wrap each in Saran Wrap to keep them clean and to retard drying out over time. Store away from sunlight (I use a shoe box). You now have 42" of good face cane 1" in diameter, and that means many hundreds of slices! The leftover ends of the face cane and the individual facial feature components can be used as background clay or to make other canes.

Just a sampling of what you can do with face canes.

A floral (rose) cane made with leftover lip segments.

Hair Canes

Striped canes can mimic wood and ivory.

Hair canes begin like stripes (straight hair) or spirals (curly hair). I don't try to build any sort of style into the hair canes. I make both straight and curly canes in color groupings like blonde, brunette, red, and black, then use slices and portions of slices to "do" the hair. (Hair can be any color you like – purple, pink, aquamarine – whatever!)

Use the hair color and a contrasting color (black or brown for light hair, white or silver for dark hair) to build the layers for hair canes. Stack the layers and leave as is or shape one end of the cane into a triangle cane for straight hair.

Roll the stripes to form a spiral and reduce some of it to form curls of different sizes. Bend a piece of the stripe back and forth onto itself to form wave canes. Cut small sections of the straight striped cane and butt them together at an angle to form a braid cane.

When ready to "dress" face canes with a hairstyle, cut and place the hair cane pieces as desired. Use bits of the hair cane to cover up any parts of the face that are not perfect. For example, if one eye isn't quite right, cover it with a "peek-a-boo" style, long bangs, or a strategically placed curl or a piece of clay for a hat brim. Forehead too low? Change the appearance with bangs and a bouffant, making the forehead invisible.

Striped canes can also be used to form feathers for decorating hats or to make angels, fairies, wings, and clouds. They also mimic wood and ivory very effectively. Build a stack with white ranging to a very light gray for the shading effect. Round one end of the feather stack and lightly compress the other.

Wrap with a thin layer of black and reduce one third of the cane for smaller feathers. Reduce the feathers to the desired finished size before building a wing cane so further reduction is not required.

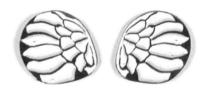

Wings and clouds made with striped stacks. Clouds are rolled up stripes, and each feather in the wing is a striped stack too!

Striped canes used for hair around face canes.

TECHNIQUES: SCULPTING, MAKING MOLDS, TRANSFERS, GRAPHIC APPLICATIONS

SCULPTING A FACE

Note: *Before starting, read the section on face canes (pages 40-44) that pertains to the placement and proportions of features. You will find it helpful here as well.*

You will need

2 oz. well-conditioned clay

Making the face

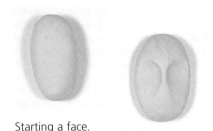

Starting a face.

1. Roll a ball of clay into an oval. Faces can be round, oval, or even very elongated. (I usually go for somewhere in between, as pulls from the mold can always be stretched and manipulated to make each face different.)

2. Press the clay oval down on the worktable. Use the inner curve of your palm to flatten it slightly, but maintain a rounded surface.

3. Use your two index fingers or thumbs to indent hollows for the eyes not quite halfway down the length of the face, leaving space for a nose in between.

Add the nose.

4. Roll a small piece of clay into a wedge or teardrop shape. Make it slightly larger than the final nose, as some will spread when you apply it. Place the nose shape on the center of the face and spread the top bit across the forehead to the right and left, using two fingers to smooth it out from the center. Smooth the nose

wedge onto the face down along the sides of the nose. Eliminate any creases with your fingers or shaping tools. You can add little balls of clay for nostrils on either side of the nose at the bottom. (I didn't in this version.)

5. Smooth all the skin surfaces. Look at the head from the side as well as from the front, and make sure the nose is shaped in a way that pleases you. Do this now so you won't have to adjust it after the eyes are in place.

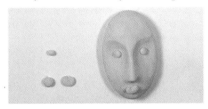

Add the eyeballs and mouth.

6. Roll two small eyeballs and place them in the eye socket indentations.

7. Form the lips by rolling a slightly larger ball. Flatten it just a bit and use your fingernail to indent slightly in the center, forming a flat-bottomed heart shape. Position this in the mouth area, under the nose with a little room in between. Press it lightly in place. Use the back of a knife blade or an X-acto blade to form two lips in the middle of the mouth. Extend the line just slightly past the lips onto the face. Curve upward at the outside corners just slightly. (You can always add more expression and detail later using the pulls from your mold.)

Add the upper and lower eyelids.

8. For the upper eyelids, roll a larger ball, flatten it, and cut it in

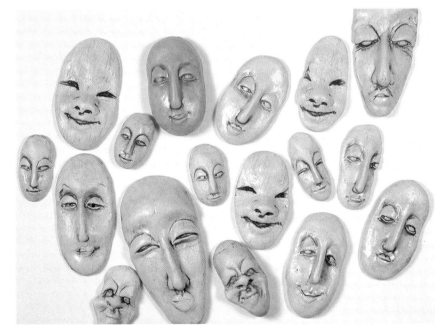

Above. Baked and stained faces.

Opposite. Sarajane Helm. "Ivory Maiden" collage.

half. Curve each piece up slightly over the end of your finger and pinch the corners of the half-circle just a little to form a crescent shape. Apply these over the eyeballs in the eye sockets. The straight edge goes across the eye opening and the rounded part should fit nicely into the hollow of the eye socket.

9. Roll out very thin clay snakes to be the lower eyelids. Cut two equal pieces, roll very slightly at the ends to taper them, and use a toothpick to carefully place them under the eyes. Use a tool to gently stroke the clay in place, as you did with the nose. Blend the curve of the upper eyelid into the eye socket as well.

10. Smooth any rough skin surfaces. Slightly indent the oval of the face at the temples (out from eyes).

11. Bake the face according to package directions for 30 minutes. This baked face can now be used to make a mold. Read on!

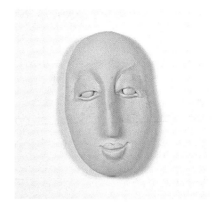
The finished face, ready to mold.

MAKING A FACE MOLD

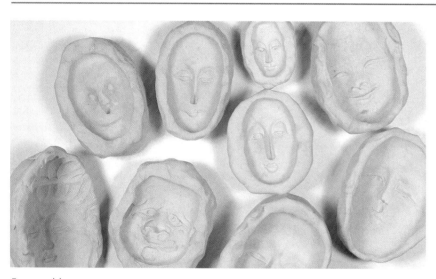
Face molds.

You will need

2 oz. Super Elasticlay
original baked polymer face
talcum powder or cornstarch

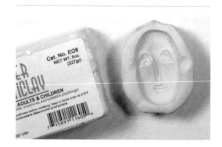
Super Elasticlay and the face impression.

Making the mold

1. Powder the original baked clay face thoroughly, including the edges. Make sure the powder is in the eyes and nose of the face but avoid powdering so vigorously that you get it in your eyes and nose! (You don't want to breathe particulate matter, even cornstarch or talcum powder, so wield the brush gently.) Ponce bags work very well on flat surfaces, but faces and other original pieces with depth should be powdered with a brush.

2. Knead the Elasticlay until it's warm and pliable. It is much softer than most clays, and takes an impression beautifully.

3. Make a ball bigger than the original baked clay face. Slightly flatten it on the work surface.

4. Press the original baked face into the oval of clay, face down. Press straight down, not at an angle. The clay ball should be large enough so that when the original face is pressed in it, there is still clay under the nose. Don't press the face so far into the clay that it pokes through the bottom. There should also be clay around all the edges.

5. Pull the Elasticlay up to meet the outside edges of the original, forming a nice solid mold wall. If you have lots of excess, trim some off at this point.

6. Ease the walls open slightly. Use your fingernails on the very top of the exposed original, at the temple area (slightly above the midline), to grip and pull the original face straight out. Any indents left by your fingers will look like temples. (If this pulling action proves too difficult, glue a plug of baked clay, a strip of leather, or a pin back finding to the back of the face and use that as a handle to remove the original from the clay.) Try to pull straight out in one movement, so as not to distort the impression. If it is difficult to pull out the original, it may mean that you didn't use enough powder.

7. Slide a knife carefully under the mold to release it from the work surface and place it in a baking pan. If this causes distortion that you can't adjust, make the mold again and form it directly in the baking pan. Or make the molds on index file cards or other small squares of cardstock and move it along with this base.

8. Check the mold. If it's not absolutely clean and precise, wad up the Elasticlay, repowder your original, and try again. This only takes a few minutes, which are well spent to get a mold that can be used for years. Take care to make it the best you can. I get very picky about the details at this stage. It pays off in ease of use later.

9. Some people bake the originals in the mold, but you can't check for a clean impression that way, and sometimes the original and the mold become fused. Bake the Elasticlay mold for 15 to 30 minutes in a 275°F oven. Do not overbake.

10. Remove the mold from the oven and allow it to cool completely. The mold is still very pliable when warm, so resist the temptation to poke it to see if it's done.

Using the mold

1. Copies of the original face (sometimes called "pulls") can now be made very easily. Powder the mold with a brush. Don't overpowder and make sure powder doesn't collect in the nose or other hollows.

2. Condition some clay until it is warm and pliable.

3. Roll out a thick snake and cut a chunk about as big as the original face. If the clay overflows the mold area, use a smaller piece. If you don't use enough, you will get only part of the face (which can be very interesting) or you will get a pull that is too shallow to keep its shape well. Experiment until you find the right size lump. You may want to cut several pieces and make several at once.

4. Roll the conditioned clay chunk into a smooth ball and press it into the mold. Make sure enough clay gets into the nose area. If necessary, start with a teardrop-shaped

wad and stick the tip into the nose cavity, then press the rest of the clay into the mold. Use your fingers to press the clay firmly into all parts of the mold, making sure the clay is evenly distributed. Press another wad of clay into the back of the piece in the mold, and use it to remove the pull (you can see why it's called this). The Elasticlay mold is still flexible after baking and cooling, and you can use this flexibility to pop the pieces out, especially if the mold is well powdered. (Molds do tend to harden with age.)

5. Smooth the surfaces and edges of all pulls as needed. Change the expressions if you like, or reshape the face completely by pulling or pushing different parts. Make it long and thin by pulling the forehead and chin lengthwise, or fatten it up by pushing the forehead and chin toward the center a bit, then pulling the face outwards through the cheek and features area. Add eyebrows, a mole, or other details. Use a toothpick or knife blade to change the mouth and eyes to add individual expression. Play with the face and see what's possible. This will spark more ideas (and those that don't work, you can wad up and try again!).

Stain brings out the details and changes the look.

6. Bake these pulls according to the clay package directions for 30 minutes. You can stain them or add details with acrylic paints. You can also use powdered chalk or powdered face makeup to color them before baking, or use Prismacolor pencils or felt tip pens to color them after baking.

Note: *You can add further clay "dressing" and embellishments before you bake the faces, but I prefer to bake the faces first, then rebake assemblages. This not only keeps the unbaked faces from getting marred or smashed, it also allows me to stain, antique, or color the entire face piece, then drape clay over the features. It's much harder to color them in afterwards.*

This draped face pendant is ready to string with coordinating beads.

The "Snowflake Princess" pin makes use of snowflake cutters and a molded face.

Photocopies of pictures can be transferred to clay. (Transfer photo original by Greg Anderson.)

Using photocopies and photos with polymer clay is a lot of fun! Many laser printers use toner that will not transfer, but simple photocopies are often compatible with clay use. It takes a little experimentation, but once you find a machine with inks that transfer, you can make black and white copies of any copyright-free images, drawings, or family pictures. This is a particularly good way to use very old photos without harming the original.

Applying a transfer

1. Roll out a sheet of clay on a piece of paper or cardstock. The paper will help you later to get the piece off the work surface without damaging the image.

2. Make photocopies the desired size and place the paper, image side down, on the clay sheet.

3. Burnish the paper on the clay sheet to make sure all parts are touching. Allow this to sit for 10 to 30 minutes. The plasticiser from the clay will melt the toner/inks and transfer them to the clay. (Remember doing something like this with newspaper and Silly Putty?)

4. Bake the clay with the paper still in place.

5. Remove from the oven and let cool slightly. Pull the paper off before the piece has cooled completely.

6. If desired, color the transferred image with Prismacolor felt tip pens or pencils. Transferred images don't need to be glazed to protect the image, but can be coated if you like the effect.

Using photos on clay

You can also use photos, both prints and Polaroids, directly with polymer clay. Roll a sheet of clay on an index card or cardstock and cut the image to fit. Place the photo face up on the clay. Hold it in place and cover the edges of the picture by applying small pieces of clay to secure the picture. Bake right away – if you let these sit too long, the plasticiser in the raw clay can soak through the pictures and mar them.

Photos can be baked at the same temperature as the clay.

CREATING CARDS, WRAPPING PAPER, AND MORE

Greeting cards using polymer clay art are fun to make. Stamps can be used to change the look of a printed card, or use polymer clay embellishments.

Greeting and note cards, wrapping paper, t-shirt transfers, and more can be made using images of polymer clay artwork.

Make cards by gluing thin slices of canes or impressed pieces to folded cardstock. I use white PVA glue such as Aleene's or Sobo to affix polymer clay to paper. Glue a single snowflake, heart, or star to a piece of brightly colored cardstock for a simple and unique card. Thin pieces of clay will not create a postal problem. If you want the clay piece to be removable, hold it in place with a small dot of glue in the center only. When the piece is made as a flat and lightweight ornament, it can be both a card and a gift!

If you have a computer, scan a photo or take a digital photo of your favorite polymer piece and save it as a file in your computer. Most computers come with a graphics program already installed. I like Adobe Photoshop for the many adjustments and effects it allows. When scanning or shooting digitally, save the photos at 300 dpi (dots per inch) so as to be able to have print-quality resolution. This makes for a large file, but also for a good print later. (Just because an image looks large and lovely on your screen does not mean it will look the same when printed.)

Import the file into any readily available (and relatively inexpensive) program such as Broderbund's Print Shop. I found this program on sale at the local office supply store for less than $30, and it is widely available through stores nationwide. It's just one of many such programs now available.

Using the templates built into the program, a home computer user with little or no training can create amazing works of art. This is not only an incredible tool to have for personal items such as invitations, cards, address labels, etc., it is a great boon to the professional who wishes to sell their work. Make business cards, flyers, promotional and advertising materials of all kinds, for a fraction of the cost. You can try out 20 different designs until you find one that is just right and change it again at a moment's notice, without having to order (and pay for!) 1,000 copies.

PROJECTS FOR SPRING

*"And in the green underwood and cover
Blossom by blossom the spring begins."*
-Algernon Swinburne

WHEN THE GRIP OF WINTER'S COLD BEGINS TO

ease and signs of new life emerge once again upon the land, we see the signs of renewal all around us. We can feel it internally too, if we pay attention. The sight of flowers and buds on the branches that were formerly bare is a powerful reminder that the sap is rising and that new beginnings are possible in many ways. Things that had seemed completely dormant begin growing anew! Symbols of life and creative energies resonate as a force in ourselves, and we feel new vigor. Spring is the time of new life, of the first flowers that push up from the ground while the snow still melts, and the profusion in nature that follows. A time of fresh green shoots and baby birds, animals, and people too. We celebrate many holidays in Spring that have to do with new and renewed life. Mothers and infants, eggs and chicks, baby animals of all sorts, and seeds that sprout to new growth – all these are symbols of the promise of continuing life we find in each Spring.

Opposite. "Spring Collage" features cane slices by: Sarajane Helm, Leigh Ross, Dawn Naylor, Donna Kato, Nancy Osbahr, Janet Scheetz, Tamila Darling, Layl McDill, Stefanie Wagner, Mary-Lu Elliot, Ellen Berne, Candace Mathewson, Marie Segal, and Hema Hibbert.

Vernal Equinox:
Spring Flowers Boxed Set

The Spring Flowers Boxed Set, cards, and jewelry. The box lid is decorated with a polymer sheet made from a variety of cane slices pressed into a clay base.

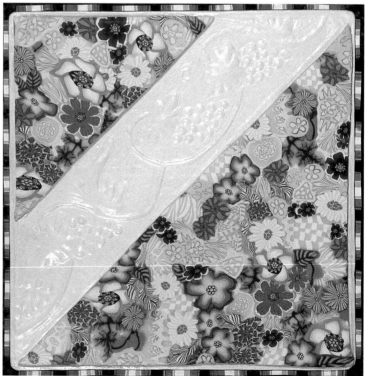

The box lid. The box features a grapevine design pressed into the papier mâché, so I simply painted that part.

This boxed set combines the powers of polymer clay and the personal computer. To make the floral canes, I used my scanner to capture images from my garden. As the flowers bloomed, I brought a sample of each inside and placed it on the computer scanner bed with a sheet of ivory colored cardstock on top. Then I used the "import" command in my graphics program to capture a high resolution (300 dpi) image file in the tiff format, which I stored on a disc for convenience. (I also store all images as jpg files and use those if I want to play around with filters or effects without changing the original image.)

I used simple color printouts of cosmos and marigolds as references, along with templates found in Broderbund's Printshop program to design and print floral greeting cards. This program allows you to import your own graphics as well as use a huge array of clip art, borders, frames, and backgrounds. You can add words in all shapes and sizes, and color them to fit your theme and purpose. I also made business card size pieces in the vertical layout option that could be folded over and stapled to bags of seeds for each kind of plant. I collected the seeds later in the year (keep in mind that some projects take several seasons to complete).

Personalized greeting and note cards can be printed on plain white or colored cardstock, but be aware that printing on a colored background changes the colors of the final images. You can also use glossy cardstock. Most office supply stores carry kits with cardstock and matching envelopes in a variety of paper and cardstock types. Scans of natural images such as flowers can be combined or overlaid with polymer clay images and used to great effect. A scan of translucent canes by Leigh Ross was used to make the Thank You card shown in the photo. Polymer clay images scanned in the computer can be cut and pasted into different templates to make stationery, address labels, calling cards, and more. You can also incorporate images of polymer clay artwork taken with a digital camera.

The "Spring Flowers" box began as a brown papier mâché box that came to me years ago. I knew it would be a wonderful background for further beautification, and saved it until the right project came along. It is just the right size to hold cards and envelopes. When a roll of stamps and address labels are tucked inside, along with a complete set of the flower and herb seeds I collected and bagged, the box makes a fabulous springtime gift. Plant the seeds of a friendship that will keep on blooming. Or bring new blooms to a friend you already enjoy!

Approximate size:

6" x 6" x 3"

You will need

papier mâché box
acrylic paint
Flecto Varathane or gesso
2 oz. white polymer clay
lace cane (see page 32 for making instructions)
floral cane (see page 33 for making instructions)
leaf cane (see page 39 for making instructions)
decorative square cane (see page 38 for making instructions)

Decorating the Spring Flowers Box

1. Paint the outside of a papier mâché box and lid with a mixture of acrylic paint and varathane or gesso. Use the varathane or gesso instead of water to thin the paint. Add enough to make a creamy, workable consistency and check the paint color on a scrap sheet of paper first. This mixture seals and protects the paper box as well as adds color and gloss. I chose an ivory color made by mixing white and a little yellow. I used a 1" wide brush and gave it several coats, allowing it to dry completely between coats. If desired, you can paint the inside of the box and lid or glue decorative paper or fabric as a liner. (Recycled yogurt containers make wonderful paint containers and allow you to store the paint mix for a few days. Sometimes you'll need to do touchups after you've finished painting.)

2. This particular box features a pressed grapevine design in the papier mâché, going across the middle of the lid and around the sides of the box. I left these areas exposed since the grapevine pattern is quite attractive. On the box lid, on either side of the grapevine strip, there are raised lines that form and outline two triangular areas on the box lid. I used a piece of plain white paper to trace these triangular areas and cut out a template for each. If the box you are using has no design, make a paper template of the box lid shape.

3. Condition a 2 oz. block of white clay (substitute a color if you prefer).

4. Roll the clay through a pasta roller at a #4 setting or by hand to a thickness of around 1/16" to create a sheet large enough to accommodate the paper triangle templates with a bit of room to spare. After making sure the clay sheet is big enough, set the paper templates aside.

Lace cane slices.

5. Cut thin slices of a lace cane made with white and translucent clays. They can be very simple and still be quite effective. The thinner the slices, the better the effect. Group some of the slices together and scatter them across the base clay sheet. Leave some areas open to apply floral and leaf canes.

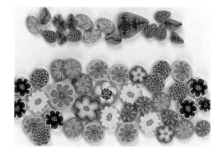

Leaf and floral cane slices.

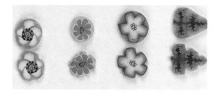

Trim the excess background away from the cane slices with a pointed cutter.

6. Cut thin slices of leaf and floral canes. Use the point of a star or other shaped cookie cutter to remove the background clay from between the petals and leaf sections. If you used translucent as the background fill when making the canes, removing some of it now will make the images very easy to layer.

7. Place a few leaf cane slices on the base clay sheet and top with a flower cane slice to make it look as though the leaves are behind the flower. Or cut cane slices into pieces and place them alongside others to create the illusion of depth. Place flowers, leaves, and lace cane slices as desired, then use a clean rod or roller to press all the slices firmly in place. Keep rolling to meld them all together. You can put this sheet through the pasta roller using a #1 setting, then a number #3 setting, if you are careful to use a clean machine or put a layer of plastic wrap across the top of the clay sheet for protection. You may need to trim the sheet to fit the width of the pasta machine.

8. After a sheet is formed, smooth it with your fingers to eliminate any fingerprints. Place the paper triangle templates on the clay sheet and use a knife to cut them out.

9. Carefully place the triangular clay pieces on a paper-lined baking tray. Make sure they are laying completely flat and that the paper templates still fit (sometimes the clay stretches when moved). Trim or reposition if needed.

10. Follow the clay manufacturer's instructions and bake for 30 minutes. Let the clay cool slightly. Use white PVA glue such Aleene's or Sobo to affix the still-warm polymer clay triangles in position on the papier mâché box lid. Remove any excess glue around the edges, then place a heavy book on top to hold everything in place while the glue dries.

11. Cut enough slices from a decorative square cane to cover the four edges of the box lid and bake the cane slices according to package directions. Allow them to cool.

12. Tip the lid on one edge and glue the baked slices of decorative square canes around the rim. Turn and repeat for all four sides, allowing drying time in between. After five minutes or so check each side and press the tiles in place as needed to make a neat join to the box with each.

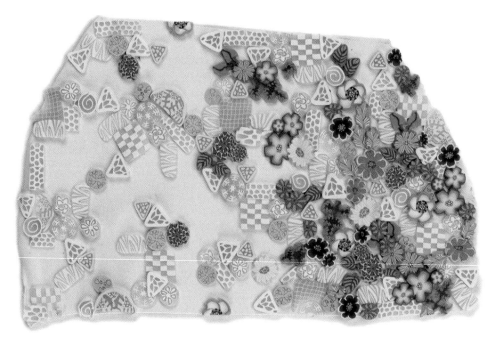

A base layer of white clay scattered with a variety of lace, floral, and leaf cane slices.

Mardi Gras:
Miniature Masks

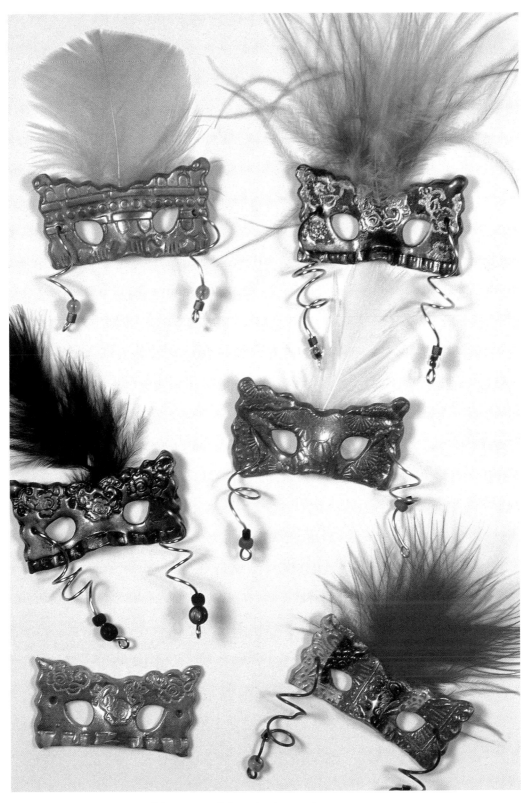

Miniature Mardi Gras domino masks.

Masks have served ceremonial purposes throughout time. Masks allow us to hide and to flaunt at the same time. We capture the representation of life forms and spirits both familiar and very different and make them part of ourselves. Animal or human, fey creature or fanciful being, masks represent far more than mere decoration. Whether used in ancient religious rites or cultural theater, masks range from raw simplicity of decoration and form to the wildly embellished and gilt encrusted treasures out of the hands of master artisans and crafters. Many are found in museum collections around the world.

Masks serve to remind us that there are layers upon layers, and many times the visible face is different than the one beneath; change is always possible. There is a great deal of magic in that thought, and that is why masks are such a strong tool for the actor and the shaman both! Masks are traditionally used during Mardi Gras, Halloween, and Purim. They can be worn as costume components or used in decorating. The endless styles possible make it easy to add wonderful displays to walls.

Miniature masks can also be used in decorative ways, as elements in larger collage pieces or framed collections. They can be worn as jewelry as pins or pendants. By changing the colors and the stamps or other objects used to make the impressions, you can vary the look considerably. Try it with different cookie cutters as your original form, or free cut with a craft or X-acto knife.

Approximate Size:
2" to 3"

You will need

2 oz. block black polymer clay (enough for several masks)
PearlEx powders (Misty Lavender, Flaming Pink, Aztec Gold)
small amount of gold leaf
colored wire
small beads
feathers
texture plates, rubber stamps (I used Lace Pointe #121808 and Flora Corner #12180-B2 from Uptown Design)
pliers
wire cutter
cardboard tube
fluted-edge circle (biscuit/cookie) cutter (2" to 3")
small teardrop-shaped Kemper tool cutter
Flecto Varathane
Super Glue
1" x 1/4" leather strip (if making pendant)

Making a half-circle miniature mask

1. Condition the black clay well and roll it through the pasta roller at the #3 setting or by hand to about 1/8" thick.

The overlarge half-circle cut out of the black clay sheet.

2. Cut a strip with one straight edge. The straight edge is the bottom of the mask. Use the circle cutter to cut slightly more than a half circle. Smooth the edges and the clay surface with your finger.

3. Use the teardrop cutter to cut eyeholes with the point of the teardrop facing the sides of the mask. Position them about 1/4" above the bottom edge of the mask and about the same distance from the sides. There should be space between them for the nose. Remove the cutout eyeholes.

4. Press the clay onto a texture plate or rubber stamp, especially on the brow, cheek and nose areas.

5. Use a needle tool to poke holes between the eyeholes and the outside edges on both sides of the mask for the wires that will be added later.

Form the nose with your finger, then add powders to the impressed areas.

6. Place your fingertip under the mask to gently raise the nose area, forming a slight rise.

7. Place the mask over a cardboard tube to round it slightly.

8. Remove it from the cardboard tube and use your clean fingertip to very carefully apply small amounts of PearlEx powders to the raised areas as desired. You can use metallic powders, or "interference" colors, which change with the direction of the light (like dichroic glass).

Gold foil on black clay to make a frill.

9. Make a frill by applying gold leaf to a small wad of black clay, then running it through the pasta roller at the #6 setting or by hand to 1/32" thick to get a crackle effect from the leaf.

10. Pinch folds along the bottom edge to form a ruffle. Use your thumbnail or a small cutter to remove the excess clay from the folded area.

11. Pick up the mask and gently press the frill in place behind the top area of the mask. Press carefully along the edge of the mask so you don't distort the raised areas.

12. Use your fingertip to add gold or other color powders on the frill and mask as desired. Carefully rim the eyeholes with powder.

13. Place the mask back on the cardboard tube, reshaping if needed, and bake in a preheated oven at 270°F or according to the package instructions, for 30 minutes.

14. When cool, apply a coat of varathane with a small brush and allow it to dry completely.

15. Brush clean with water and allow to dry.

16. When dry, glue a feather on the back side of the mask. You may have to cut the feather down to get a good look for your mask (don't overpower a small mask with a too-large feather).

17. Use wire cutters to cut two 3" lengths of colored wire. With pliers, shape a small loop at one end and slip two or three small beads on the wires. Shape curls by bending the wires around a knitting needle or X-acto knife handle.

18. Insert the wires into the holes in the mask and bend to form a closed loop on each.

Domino Mask Variation

Instead of using a circle cutter, this mask's top edge was cut with a star-shaped cutter. Use just two of the points of the star to cut a piece of clay. The process is the same as for the Mardi Gras Half-Circle Mask. I used rubber stamp Peony Curl #121802 from Uptown Design to stamp along the upper edge. For the ruffled effect along the bottom, I pressed the bottom edge of the mask into the fluted side of the cookie cutter. As further embellishment, you could glue a row of polyester lace to the back of the mask along the edge, string some tiny beads between the eye holes, or touch up the feather lightly with glitter glue.

Easter:
Millefiore Cane Covered and Filigree Eggs

Eggs are a symbol of life and fertility around the world. Their rounded form is pleasing to the eye and to the touch. Eggs are dyed with a wax resist process to make traditional Hungarian and Romanian Pysanki. Eggs can be simply colored or lavishly encrusted with splendid and costly details, as in the Faberge versions, which were made of precious metals and gemstones for the delight of the artist's royal patrons. Now eggs can be decorated with polymer clay in these and other styles too numerous to mention here – they really deserve a book all their own.

When emptied of their contents and allowed to dry, chicken, duck, or goose eggshells form an "egg-cellent" base that can be covered with polymer clay to form sturdy ornaments and decorative objects for Easter or other holidays. A thin base layer of clay is applied to the eggs and baked, then a decorative outer layer of clay is applied. The base layer makes it easy to smooth the outer layer without cracking the egg.

Small, medium, large, or extra-large – all eggs have their uses and all are good to cover with polymer clay. The finished egg will be larger than the raw shell. (No matter which you choose, the egg comes first!)

In the course of blowing out dozens of eggs, I found the way that works best for me. This helps avoid popping your ears or sinuses too! If you do this every time you make quiche, cookies, or a nice family-sized omelet, you can build up quite a stockpile of empty shells without having to do dozens on the same day.

To blow eggs, you will need

raw eggs
pointed metal pick, large needle, or
   paring knife
large needle or long piece of wire
bowl

Blowing eggs

1. Rinse the eggs under hot water and wash the needle or wire before using it to avoid contamination.

2. Over a bowl in an easily cleaned area, hold the egg with the larger rounded end up and use the metal pick to delicately chip at the center of the round area to form a small hole in the shell. Center the hole as well as you can, especially if you are going to hang the eggs later. Tap the edges of the hole slightly to enlarge it as needed. Don't try to break through in a single jab or you may crack the entire shell.

3. Insert a clean large needle or piece of wire into the egg and stir it around to break the sac and eliminate clumping. Don't poke through the other side of the egg yet.

4. Turn the egg over with a bowl underneath. With the pointy end of the egg now up, tap a hole in the center of this end as you did on the other end.

5. To blow out the contents of the egg, put your mouth around the egg. The pointy end allows a better "lip-lock" for more effective pressure. Puff up your cheeks with air and blow using that air – this reduces pressure in your ears and sinuses. As you blow into the egg, the contents should come out easily. If not, stir again with the needle and try again. Continue blowing until the egg is empty.

6. Wipe the egg with a paper towel and allow it to dry overnight or for several days. I store my blown eggs in the carton.

To cover the egg with a clay base, you will need

blown, dried egg
1 oz. scrap clay
knife
bamboo skewer
baking pan

Covering the egg with clay

1. Make a long thin strip of clay using a pasta roller set at #5 or #6 or roll by hand to a thickness of 1/24".

A clay strip cut to fit the egg.

2. Use a knife to cut a strip wide enough to fit the egg.

Wrap the strip around the egg.

Close the seam.

3. Carefully wrap the clay strip around the middle of the egg.

4. When it overlaps, press the clay lightly onto the piece underneath to mark it, then cut it at that point. Fit

the ends neatly together around the egg and smooth the join.

Form darts at the top and bottom of the egg.

5. Fold the clay in over the ends of the eggs as shown, fitting the clay like darts over the egg top and bottom.

Trim off the excess.

6. Using a knife, gently pare away the raised portions and fill in any patches as needed, using a bit of the leftover scrap clay.

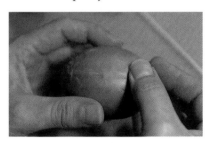

Smooth all joins and eliminate any air bubbles.

7. Use your fingers and a rod or roller to smooth the clay over the entire egg. Poke any trapped air bubbles to release them.

8. Use a bamboo skewer to poke the clay out of the holes if you want to keep them open for hanging later. (It's easy to lose track of where they are.)

9. Continue to roll and smooth the clay until there are no lumps. It doesn't need to be perfect, but you do want a good surface. Minor imperfections will be hidden – but not large ones!

A bamboo skewer inserted in the holes.

10. Insert a bamboo skewer into the egg. Carefully remove the skewer, then reinsert it all the way through from the other end. You want to have inward-going holes on both ends, but if a little clay is pushed out it can be sanded off later.

Ready for baking.

11. Thread the egg onto a bamboo skewer and suspend it over a baking pan as shown. Bake according to the clay package directions for 20 minutes.

These clay-covered eggs are very hard and durable. Now you can press thin layers of decorative clay onto the eggs and use far more pressure to smooth the clay without breaking the shell. For the Filigree Egg in the photo below, I applied purple polymer clay over the base layer, and for the Millefiore Egg I applied cane slices to the base layer.

Filigree Egg

You will need

blown egg covered with base layer
    and baked (see page 61 for instructions)
2 oz. purple clay
2 oz. Premo Gold clay
gold metallic leaf
rubber stamp, mold, texture plate,
    or other texture source
blade
powder/ponce bag
Flecto Varathane
dark stain mixture
rag
bamboo skewer
baking tray
1200-grit wet/dry sandpaper

Decorating the egg

1. Condition the purple clay well and roll it through a pasta roller at the #1 setting or by hand to a thickness of 1/8".

Apply metal leaf to the clay.

2. Add gold leaf to the top of the clay, then fold and reroll the clay several times to break up the metal leaf and distribute it throughout the clay. This is a more subtle effect than using the leaf just on the surface.

3. Roll the clay through a pasta roller set at #4 or #5 or by hand to a thickness of 1/20". Cut a strip to fit the egg and wrap it around the middle of the egg. Apply like the base layer. I used purple, but you can use

Wrap the egg with the purple/metal leaf clay strip.

any color. Smooth the join and the rest of the clay repeatedly with your fingers or an acrylic rod or brayer. (You can also use a small glass jar, but be careful when using glass to make sure it is thick enough to withstand pressure.) Carefully roll the egg between the palms of your hands for extra smoothness.

4. When it is smooth, with no obvious lumps, insert a bamboo skewer in the holes at each end of the egg so no clay protrudes from the holes. Run the skewer through both blow holes and leave the egg on the skewer.

5. Make the filigree overlays by pressing conditioned gold clay lumps onto rubber stamps or into molds or texture sheets. Be sure to powder the

Press gold clay into a mold to create a filigree design.

Let the under layer show through in places.

Wipe stain off the raised surfaces.

stamps or molds before pressing the clay. The pressings will create designs that protrude above the surface of the clay. These pieces can be sliced off using a blade held parallel to the surface of the clay.

Slice the raised image away very carefully.

6. Powder the blade and carefully cut across the surface to shave the raised design from the lump of clay.

Start in the center and apply designs to the egg surface.

7. Place the design on the work surface, then transfer it (this requires much care) with a toothpick or knife tip to the egg surface. Place the first design in the center and work with one piece at a time to build up a pattern that covers the surface, leaving some portions of the purple clay visible. Make sure all the edges of the overlay pieces adhere to the surface of the egg.

8. Use care to touch the egg as little as possible by holding the skewer instead of the egg. When you are satisfied with the design, bake the egg on the skewer for 30 minutes according to the clay package directions.

Note: *If you wish to close the holes, before baking, remove the egg from the skewer and cover the holes with a tiny amount of clay (just enough to patch the hole). Bake the egg on a nest of polyester batting or fiberfill.*

Apply varathane to the under layer.

9. After baking and cooling, brush a coat of varathane on the areas of purple clay. Allow to dry for 30 minutes.

Antique the egg with stain.

10. Antique the egg with dark stain (see the recipe on page 25). Rub the stain on the surface with your fingers or use a firm paintbrush to push

the stain into crevices and indentations.

11. Wipe off the excess stain with an old rag.

Sand lightly, then buff with a cloth.

12. Allow the egg to dry, then use 1200-grit wet/dry sandpaper to lightly sand the surface. Buff with a soft cloth to further polish the surface.

13. Make a hanger if desired from wire or ribbon. Bend the wire in a loop such as are used at the top of glass Christmas ornaments, and ease it into the egg. Or thread ribbon all the way through and loop it back, then knot to hold. Add tassels or other embellishments as desired.

Millefiore Cane Covered Egg

You will need

clay-covered eggshell (see page 61)
several inches of millefiore cane
Flecto Varathane
bamboo skewer
baking pan
blade

Decorating the egg

1. Any millifiore cane can be used to cover eggs. This example uses a chrysanthemum cane, but you can use any canes. You can even use several kinds and mix-and-match for an interesting patchwork effect. Slices are applied directly to the baked base clay covered egg.

Cut even slices of cane.

2. Use a very sharp blade to cut thin, even slices of cane. Try to make them about approximately 1/16" thick. The number needed will depend on the diameter of the cane and the size of the egg being covered.

3. Start applying the cane slices around the hole at the large rounded end of the egg.

Apply the first cane slice at the top of the egg.

Apply cane slices all around the egg.

4. Add cane slices all around the egg, leaving small spaces as needed to fit them together neatly.

Cut out small bits of background.

5. Use a small cutter with points, such as a triangle or star, to cut out small triangles from extra cane slices. These triangular pieces fit well into the blank spaces. Fill in thoroughly all around, trying not to overlap (which makes raised portions that you don't want).

6. Use a roller to begin the smoothing process, then roll the egg between your palms. Keep rolling, smoothing, and petting with your fingers until the egg is smooth. You may need to allow it to cool periodically as you work.

Fill, then smooth.

7. Thread the egg on a skewer for baking and check for fingerprints or surface irregularities. Smooth it more as needed (time spent smoothing raw clay saves sanding time later). Bake according to package directions for 30 minutes and let it cool.

Apply varathane after baking for a gloss finish.

8. After baking, use 1200-grit wet/dry sandpaper and a bowl of water to sand the egg, then buff it to a soft sheen or coat it with varathane for a high-gloss finish.

Add tassels or other embellishments to finished eggs.

May Day:
Queen of the May

This May Queen can be used as a pendant or a brooch by gluing on the appropriate jewelry finding. You can also incorporate it into a wall hanging or collage, decorate a mirror or picture frame, or glue it to a backing and add beads around it for the center of a truly unique piece.

Approximate Size:
4"

You will need

baked and stained face (see page 47 for making instructions)
floral canes (see page 35 for making instructions)
2 oz. purple clay
metallic gold inkpad
rubber stamp (I used Floral Heart #108545 from Uptown Design)
decorative-edge scissors
heart-shaped cutter (from the large aspic set – it measures 1-1/2" across)
artificial flowers
Super Glue
white craft glue

Making the queen

1. Roll the clay through a pasta roller set at #3 or #4 or by hand to a thickness of 1/16". Make a sheet large enough to accommodate the rubber stamp.

2. Press the rubber stamp into the gold inkpad and apply the design to the clay sheet. Until it's baked, the ink will smear easily, so be careful not to touch it while unbaked.

Cut around the design.

3. With the decorative-edge scissors, cut around the stamped design, forming a heart shape as shown.

Cut slices from a variety of floral canes.

4. Lay the inked heart on a work surface and use the heart cutter to cut a smaller heart out of the center.

5. Cut thin slices (1/16") from a variety of floral canes. I used five slices, but you can use more or fewer.

6. Place the two hearts and the cane slices in a baking pan and bake for 30 minutes according to the clay package directions. Let cool.

7. Slide the top of the larger heart over the forehead of the face. Super Glue the baked cane slices and the smaller heart in position as shown or in an arrangement you like. Use white glue to attach the artificial flowers. You could also add beads, feathers, or other embellishments as desired.

Mother's Day:
Natural Beauty Set

The May Queen is only one representation of the feminine figure found in many cultures. All of us came here through a mother, whether the relationship lasts long or is cut short. The mother/child relationship is the foundation of all others, and our bond to our mother the earth is a continuing one as well. This relationship has great emotional depth that makes it a potent symbol and as such is always of interest to artists!

Make this set of containers for the mom in your life. They are easy and quick, and look beautiful in the bath or boudoir. Fill the jars with lotion, hair gel, or bubble bath (fill these pretty containers from large bottles of your favorite brands). I make an extra-strength moisturizing hand cream with lanolin, cocoa butter, and few drops of glycerin. Just melt the ingredients (found at most drugstores) together in a glass container in the microwave for a few seconds at a time, and add a drop or two of fragrance oil if desired. When mostly cooled, pour into the jar and allow to set up. This keeps my cuticles and the skin on my hands from cracking all year round.

jars
decorative clay sheet (see page 56
    for making instructions)
circle cutter or X-acto knife
glue
pink and white clay (less than 1 oz.
    of each)
6-pointed star cutter (from the
    medium aspic set, 1" across)
heart-shaped Kemper cutter (1/4")

Decorating the jars

1. Start with clean unbreakable plastic jars. Because these jar lids are plastic, they should not be baked. Some metal or hard plastic lids might withstand the 275°F heat, but to be on the safe side, bake the decorative polymer clay pieces first, then glue them on the lids.

2. Refer to the instructions for the "Flower Boxed Set" to make the decorative clay sheet.

3. Trace a paper pattern of the jar lid, sizing it to fit neatly on top of the lid.

4. Cut out the desired number of clay circles (I did two) and use your finger to lightly smooth the edges.

5. Bake the circles on a flat sheet of cardstock in a baking pan, according to the clay directions for 30 minutes.

6. While the clay circles are still warm, coat the jar lids with glue. (Whether you use white PVA or Super Glue depends on the composition of the jar lid. Super Glue didn't work with these glossy plastic lids, but Sobo did.) Press the clay circles in place and carefully remove any excess glue. Use a phone book or other weight to hold the pieces in place until the glue dries.

Note: Two of the jars in this set were covered in this way. The third jar lid features a single polymer clay rose. (Don't be afraid to mix and match – that's what makes collections so interesting!)

The simple rose shown is made just like the frosting roses on a wedding cake. (Cake decorating books

Polymer roses are easy to make and bake. You can glue them on mirrors, boxes, jars, and more.

can be a great source of technique and inspiration.)

Roll the dark clay in a loose spiral.

7. To make a rose, start with two colors of clay. The center clay is darker than the outer petals. Roll a small strip of the darker clay in a loose spiral, pinching it together at the bottom but leaving it open at the top.

Roll balls of both clays and flatten them.

8. Use the white and pink clays to mix two shades of light pink, one

darker than the other. Roll between three and five balls of these clays.

Apply petals around the rose center.

Keep adding petals until you are satisfied with your rose.

9. Pinch the balls to flatten them and apply them around the center of the rose at the bottom of the rose base.

10. Cut the rose flat across the base to remove excess clay and make a smooth surface for a glue join.

11. To make the lace medallions that go around the rose, roll out a #4 (1/20") sheet using a small amount of white clay. Cut three pieces using the six-pointed star from the medium aspic set, or other cutters as desired. With the Kemper cutter, remove small pieces from inside the star to give a lacy effect. These are made in exactly the same way as the snowflakes on page 119. Place the medallions and the rose in the pan, and bake according to the clay package directions. Allow to cool.

12. Glue the rose to the center of the jar lid. Glue the three lace medallion pieces around the rose. You can use other cutouts and baked bits to decorate as desired.

13. Make labels for the jars with a computer or by hand using fancy colored or metallic inks and pen nibs, or felt tip calligraphy pens. Use a glue stick or paper that is already backed with adhesive to affix the labels. Apply a coat of varathane on the labels to make them water-resistant.

SPRING GALLERY

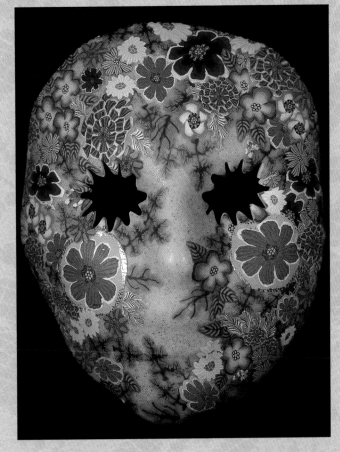

Sarajane Helm. "Spring Mask."

Photo by SnapShots.

Tamila Darling. "Pretty Posies."

Photo by Becky Green.

Becky Green and Lani Chun. "Mosaic Box."

Layl McDill. "Matilda and Mia" and detail.

Layl McDill. "Mother's Day Gardening."

Photo by Don Sweeney.

Linda Hess. "Noah and His Mrs."

Sarajane Helm. "Pins for Victoria Day!"

Bonnie Merchant. "Your Mother Should Know" Mother's Day boxes.

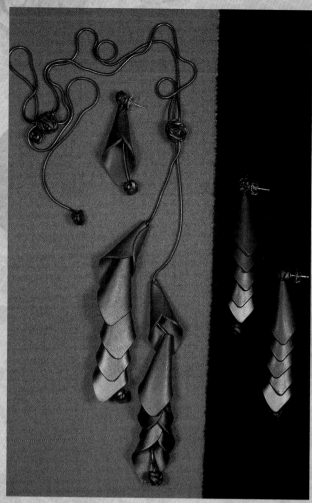

Judith Skinner. "Calla" necklace and earrings.

Olga Porteous. "Chinoise Blossom" necklace and earrings.

Dawn Naylor. Two crosses.

Jane Mahneke. "Jonquil Vase."

Deborah Anderson. "Boot With Lid."

Ellen Berne. "Mother's Day Pins."

Sandra Beach. "Sewing Basket."

Kathy Weaver. "Spring Fun Purse 2."

Kathy Weaver. "Spring Fun Purse 1."

Lisa Clarke, Polka Dot Creations.
"Three Expectant Mothers" pendants.

Robin Williams. "Baby Pins."

Sarajane Helm. "Teddy Bear and Bluebird Quilt" pin.

A basket of eggs from a swap. Includes eggs by Carol L. Simmons, Sarajane Helm, Nancy Osbahr, Sharon Olhorst, and others.

Sarajane Helm. A face bead crowned with flowers makes a great central pendant for a necklace.

Carol L. Simmons. Incredibly detailed eggs.

Sarajane Helm. Two springtime necklaces.

Sarajane Helm. Floral beads with glass and metal spacer beads.

Sarajane Helm. "Sun and Moon" eggs.

PROJECTS FOR SUMMER

"Summertime, and the livin' is easy.
Fish are jumpin', and the cotton is high"
–Summertime, Ira Gershwin

SUMMER IS THE SEASON OF WARMTH AND

abundance. It's a riotous surge toward the warmth of the growing world. Nature is at its most productive, bees are buzzing, and blossoms are quickly turning to fruits and vegetables. This is the traditional time for savoring the wide array of delights our world has to offer. The temperature is hotter at this time of year, and so are the colors! The whole range of the rainbow is available in summer, with bright tones and lots of light that changes more now than at any other time of the year. It can stream clear and crisp in the morning, golden as new honey in the hazy afternoon, or glower with the purples, yellows, and reds of impending storm clouds. Everything alive is expanding and stretching out, reaching farther, and storing away energies for the colder times that will surely come again...but not just yet, not for a while!

"Summer Collage" features cane slices by Sarajane Helm, Leigh Ross, Z Kripke, Dawn Naylor, Donna Kato, Nancy Osbahr, Janet Scheetz, Tamila Darling, Layl McDill, Stefanie Wagner, Mary-Lu Elliot, Ellen Berne, Candace Mathewson, Pamela Wynn, and Marie Segal.

Weddings:
Faux Florals

The Flower Girl's circlet, candy bowl, attendant's box, and candleholder are by Leigh Ross. The small attendant's box is a covered mint tin, which makes an excellent gift for wedding party members. Just be sure you make enough to go around, because these are gorgeous!

It's hard to believe that these flowers and foliage are made of polymer clay! Polymer artist Leigh Ross crafted the flowers and leaves and added delicate ribbons to create a charming circlet, which will certainly become a treasured keepsake.

Use the color mixablity of polymer clays to coordinate exactly with the colors the wedding party has chosen, and create a gorgeous setting for a memorable occasion. There are as many variations as your imagination can handle – different sizes of cutters, different colors, and even different numbers of petals for each flower.

Leigh has graciously shared her flower-making technique here. She and her husband Stephen Ross provided the step-by-step photos that illustrate this project.

Approximate size of one flower:

between 1-1/2" and 2-1/2" (depending on cutters)

You will need

Sculpey Super Flex clay
Premo green clay
Premo clay in flower color(s)
pastel chalks
Micro Pearl PearlEx powder
floral tape
22- or 24-gauge wire for cascading flowers and leaves
flower centers (stamens)
waxed paper
grater or crusher for chalk
clay gun
clay shapers
cookie cutters or Kemper cutters (circle shapes with fancy edgings for the main petals and/or smaller star cutters for the center and outside petals. I used the spiked flower in the butterfly cutter set and the flower from the large aspic cutter set here. Each is about 1-1/2")

Preparation

Crush the chalk.

1. Chalks: You'll need chalks in green and your choice of flower colors. Prepare the chalk by grating or crushing it into a fine powder. Add some Micro Pearl at a ratio of 4/1, chalk to PearlEx. This helps keep the chalk from clumping and makes working with it much easier.

2. Experiment with different chalk color combinations until you have the ones you want. If you choose a dark clay color for the petals, use light-colored chalk to do the shading. On light-colored petals, use a darker tone of chalk for the shading.

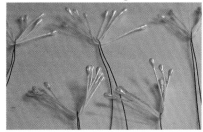
Add stamens to wires folded in half.

3. Stamens: For each flower, cut a 10" long piece of 22-gauge wire. Bend the wires in half and crimp the fold with pliers. Pull four or five stamens into the crimped fold of the wire, folding them in half in the process.

Wrap the wires with floral tape.

4. Slightly stretch the end of a 36" length of floral tape and lay the wire with the stamens on the tape. Squeeze the tape around the wire and start wrapping the tape down the length of the wire, holding the stamens in the wire. I find it easier to wrap one layer rather sparsely, then wrap a second time for good coverage. The first layer tends to be hard to grip. Set the wrapped wires aside.

5. Leaf wires: For each leaf, cut a 10" long piece of 22-gauge wire and fold it in half. Crimp the fold with pliers and set aside.

6. Clay: Condition both the Sculpey Flex and the Premo clay colors of your choice. Mix the Premo into the Sculpey Flex at a ratio of up to 50/50, depending on the colors and the effect you are looking for. If you want to keep the Sculpey Flex the original color, mix it with translucent clay. Either way, you need to add some Premo to the mix or the Sculpey Flex clay will be too crumbly to make the flowers. For this project you'll need a green clay for the leaves and colors of your choice for the flowers.

1. Separately roll the conditioned clay colors through a pasta machine to a thickness of about 1/32". Roll only enough clay for one or two flowers at a time. Put this flat sheet of clay on a piece of waxed paper to keep it from sticking to your work surface.

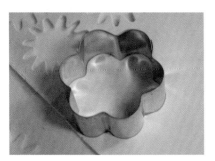

Cut petals out of rolled clay sheets.

2. Use cutters to cut out petals the shape of your choice, just like you would Christmas cookies. Cut at least four sets of petals for each flower – one small star shape for the center around the stamens, two larger sets that make up the actual flower, and another small green star that becomes the finishing piece against the bottom of the petals.

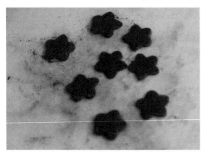

Brush chalk powder on the cutouts.

3. Pull the scrap clay off the waxed paper, leaving just the cutouts on the paper. Brush the light shade of chalk over the dark cutouts, then turn them over and apply chalk to the backs. You now have petals covered with pastel chalk. Gently roll the clay shaper on the edge of each petal, stretching the clay along its edge, ruffling the edge of the petal all the way around.

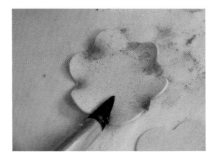

Shape the petals with a clay shaper and apply chalk powder.

4. For the light-colored clay petals, dip the clay shaper in the dark-colored chalk powder and lay the shaper on the edge of the petal. Gently roll the clay shaper on the edge of the petal, stretching the clay along its edge, ruffling the edge of the petal all the way around. You may want to dip the clay shaper in the chalk powder while you are doing this to make sure you have color all along the edge. You can also fill this in with a brush, making sure to keep the darker color on the edges.

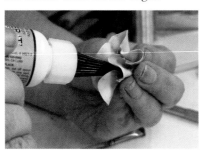

Shape the petal into a bowl shape over a plastic nozzle or pen cap.

5. Carefully pick up the clay petals and form them into a bowl shape, being careful not to tear the clay.

Bake the bowl-shaped petals.

6. Place all the petals on a baking sheet and bake them at 275°F for no more than 20 minutes. Premo clay can be baked over and over again, but Super Flex clay will lose its elasticity if it is baked more than once or baked for too long. When they are finished baking, make a small hole in the center of each petal by poking it with a toothpick or needle tool.

To make the leaves, use the petal technique with a small exception – add wire to the back before chalking that side of the leaf.

1. Roll the conditioned green clay through the pasta roller at the next to thinnest setting or by hand to a thickness of 1/32".

2. Place the rolled clay sheet on a piece of waxed paper and cut out the leaves.

3. Remove the scrap clay, leaving the leaf cutouts on the waxed paper. Dust one side of the leaves with green chalk powder.

4. Gently lift the leaves and lay them chalk side down on a clean piece of waxed paper.

5. Use a clay gun to extrude some of the green clay using the small or medium flat line disc (the one that looks like a hyphen). If you don't have a clay gun, cut thin strips from the rolled green sheet.

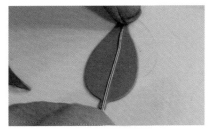

Lay the wire on the back of the leaf.

6. Lay a leaf wire down the center of each leaf.

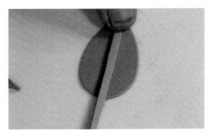

Lay a strip of green clay over the wire.

7. Lay a length of the extruded clay or a clay strip over the wire. Use

the clay shaper to smooth the edges of the added clay into the back of the leaves.

8. Dust both sides of the leaf cutout with green chalk powder.

Shape the leaf.

9. Roll the clay shaper over the edges of each leaf to stretch them slightly – not as much as you did on the petals, just enough to shape the leaves.

10. Bake the leaves on a baking sheet at 275°F for no more than 20 minutes.

Assembly

Slide the smallest petal on the wire up to the stamens.

1. Slide the smallest petal on the wire with the stamens. Glue the petal to the floral tape just where the stamens end and the floral tape begins. This makes a good stopgap for the rest of the petals. Wait until the glue dries before adding the rest of the petals.

Slide progressively larger petals on the wire, with the smaller ones nearest the stamens.

2. Add the other petals to the wire below the small petal and add the green star at the bottom. Dab a little glue on the last one, then run floral tape around the wire to the end of the wire. Use as much floral tape as necessary to secure the petals.

3. Add a small piece of floral tape around the leaf wire, starting at the end of the leaf. This helps hold the leaf on the flower.

Wrap the flower and leaf wires together.

4. Start the floral tape again on the flower wire and wrap about 3/4" of the wire, then lay the leaf wire on the flower wire and finish wrapping the two wires together. You now have a flower/leaf combination.

5. If you want to make a cascading section of flowers, take one of the flower/leaf combinations and wrap floral tape for 1", add another flower/leaf combination and continue wrapping. Every inch or so, add another flower/leaf combination until you have the length of cascading flowers you want. Finish off with floral tape to the end of the stem.

Wedding goblets, candleholders, and flowers by Leigh Ross. Leigh used translucent, ivory, copper, gold, heather purple, and green clays to create a serene and summery wedding set that is just amazing. She first created many intricate floral canes, then used them to create tightly detailed sheets of raw clay to cover a variety of glass goblets, bowls, candleholders, and more. These can be used to decorate the altar or chapel area or as table centerpieces at the reception.

The roses and leaves are all made of clay by Leigh Ross.

Leigh used gold leaf on the underside of the cane sheet applied to this bowl. It shows through the glass for a lovely effect.

A stunning polymer clay bouquet.

Summer Solstice:
Butterfly Cutouts and Canes

Pressed Butterfly Jewelry or Magnet

Use these butterflies as earrings or pins by gluing on the correct findings, or glue them on small magnets and decorate your refrigerator. A few of these glued on a plain mirror or picture frame are guaranteed to brighten up a room.

You will need

small amounts of clay in jewel tone
   colors for wings
very small amount of black clay
28-gauge black wire
gold inkpad or PearlEx powders
rubber stamp (I used Lotus
   #B31043 from Uptown Design)
butterfly cutter set (see Sources,
   page 143, Off The Beaten Path)
wire cutters
round-nose pliers
Flecto Varathane

Making the butterfly

1. Roll the colored clays through the pasta roller at the #3 setting or by hand to a thickness of 1/16". Use solid colors if you are going to use an inkpad, or use mixed colors if you are going to use PearlEx powders. (Mixed colors are sometimes too busy for effective use with stamps.)

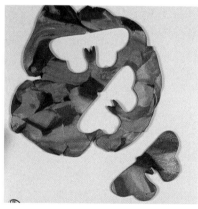

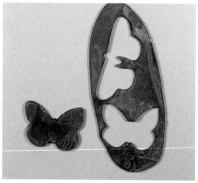

Examples of rolled clay and the wing cutouts.

Scrap clays and leftover cane ends can provide interesting color combinations, or just chop up a few different clay pieces and roll them out together. If the color spread is not pleasing, squish it up and roll it out again. Do this until you get a piece you find attractive.

Stamp the clay so the cutout wings will be symmetrical.

2. Position the butterfly cutter on the clay for the best effect and press firmly to make a clean cut. On multicolored pieces, position the cutter so there is some symmetry to the colors of the wings. With a solid colored piece, this symmetry is accomplished by stamping with the gold ink in two places. The butterfly cutter set includes eight different wing types, which provides lots of variety, especially when you change colors and embellishments.

3. If you are not using ink to stamp a design, press the raw clay wings onto a rubber stamp or other texture plate to impress the details. Lace can provide interesting texture here, as can many stamps that are not actually butterflies. Play around with all sorts and see what you like.

4. Use your fingertip to clean the edges of the cut pieces and to apply PearlEx powder to the outside edges and/or to the raised portions of the impressed designs. Be careful not to use too much powder or to touch any portions where ink was used.

5. Clean your fingers to remove any powder or ink.

The wings, body, and wire antennae.

6. Roll a very small piece of black clay for the butterfly body. Bodies are usually pointed somewhat at the top and bottom and fatter in the middle. They can be longer or shorter, depending on the type of wings you are using.

7. Press the body lightly in place between the wings and pinch the underside of the cut wing sections upward to secure them firmly to the black body section. This slightly elevates the wings and makes them look more natural.

8. Cut two pieces of wire 3/4" to 1" long for each butterfly. Use round-nose pliers to curl one end of each wire. Insert the other end into the clay at the top of the body, on either side at the head, between the wing and body layers. Push in firmly to a depth of at least 1/4". Don't wiggle them.

9. Bake the butterfly according to the clay package directions for 30 minutes. Support the butterfly wings while baking by placing them in puffs of fiberfill in the baking pan. If the wires seem unstable, add a tiny drop of glue after baking.

The butterfly after baking.

10. After baking, coat any powdered or inked parts with varathane, but don't coat the body section.

Millefiore Cane Butterfly

You can also make butterflies using millefiore caning techniques. To make this cane I used translucent and black clays. The translucent allows other clays and metallic foils to show through those sections of the wings. You can also build wing canes using colored clays instead of the translucent.

You will need

4 oz. white clay
4 oz. black clay
4 oz. translucent clay

Making wing canes and a butterfly

A wing cane in translucent and black.

1. To build the wing cane, roll translucent clay into snakes and wrap them with layers of black clay. Roll the snakes through the pasta roller at the #5 setting or by hand to a thickness of 1/24". Shape some into ovals and reduce some to a smaller scale. Use a picture of real butterfly wings to guide you in laying out the design, but don't worry if yours aren't identical. Butterfly wings usually have a group of flattened ovals fanning out and a row of small circles on the outside edges. If you make one cane and reduce it, you can cut it into four parts for the upper and lower wings, and pinch and shape the wings as you like. (You can also use the wing cane to make slices and apply to other clay just as it is, rather than building further. I cut and keep a section for that too.) The butterfly shown was made using slices of the wing cane placed around a black clay body with wire antennae, made just like the impressed butterfly but with cane slice wings.

2. Make a body section by rolling a 3" long black snake and pinching it along the top and bottom. Stand this up on your work surface like a tower with the pointed ends at the top and bottom as you look down on it.

3. Cut four pieces of wing cane, each as long as the black body section. Position two wing sections on each side of the body for the top wings. Pinch or form the other two sections slightly if desired, and place them on either side of the body to become the lower wings.

Antennae are made as spirals. Pack background clay around all the components once they are correctly placed.

4. Roll out a sheet of white clay at the #1 setting to create a piece 6" long by 2" wide. Roll out another sheet of black clay the same size but at the #5 setting or by hand to a thickness of 1/24". Place the black sheet on top of the white sheet. Roll the long edge into a jellyroll spiral with one end left free.

5. Cut into two 3" pieces to form two antennae and place them so the unrolled section joins the black body at the top, between the wings and with the jellyroll spirals curling outward.

6. Pack all the areas around the antennae, body, and wings with white background clay and reduce.

Gold leaf on back of the cane slice, placed on pink background clay and stretched carefully.

7. Cut thin slices of the cane and back them with a thicker piece of colored clay, rolling this joined piece out and stretching it to make the translucent sections even thinner. If you put a piece of gold foil on the back of the slice before applying it to colored clay, gold flecks will show through the translucent but not through the black. It is a very nice effect! You can use this complete butterfly cane to make beads, pins, and other items.

Labor Day:
Clayworker's Toolbox

On a day that honors workers and all they do, what could be a better symbol than beautiful tools? A box to keep them in, of course!

You can keep tools of all sorts in a box like this – clay tools, embroidery or beading items, sculpting, stamping, or calligraphy needs, all the essentials for a manicure, or whatever you like. Make a toolbox and fill it with goodies for a knock-your-socks-off gift. This is a great palette to use your imagination, personal taste, and existing stash of canes and decorative items.

This box began as a plain lunchbox with no screen printing or decoration, just bare metal and a red plastic handle. (I bought several from American Science and Surplus. You can also use old plastic or metal lunchboxes, but raised areas and paints may cause problems. Decorating vintage lunchboxes destroys their potential worth as a collector's item, so I recommend starting with a bare box.)

Boxes can be decorated hot or cold. The hot way is to bake the clay directly on the metal box after you remove the plastic handle. The cold way is to bake polymer items first and glue them to the box. The instructions here are for the cold method.

Approximate Size:

8-1/2" x 7" x 4"

You will need

plain metal lunchbox
stick-on business card sized magnet
dimensional fabric/craft paint (I
    used Liquid Silver Iridescent by
    Tulip)
variety of baked polymer clay tiles
baked slices from the edge of a large
    cane
baked cane slices
blue glass tiles
polymer clay face (see page 47 for
    making instructions)
polymer butterfly (see page 86 for
    making instructions)
silver metallic Beedz
tiny blue glass beads
rhinestones

Decorating the box

1. Gather all the embellishment elements together and experiment with a variety of arrangements to find a pleasing composition. This step is often skipped by the impatient among us, but choosing the right components before you start is a very important part of the end result. Take your time and play. Look at the items from different angles. Get an idea of how pieces go together before you start gluing.

2. Use the silver dimensional paint to draw curlicue lines around the front of the box. Fill the area inside the recessed area of the lid, but leave the rim bare.

3. Add decorative elements of your choice to the baked polymer face to make a medallion. I used a butterfly and impressed pieces of clay.

4. Use Super Glue to secure the polymer items to the box and white glue to affix the glass tiles in a pleasing design.

5. After the silver dimensional paint has dried completely, use the same paint to draw new lines right next to the dry lines.

6. Place the box on a sheet of newspaper and pour the tiny blue glass beads where desired on the wet paint. Allow to dry, then tap the box to remove the excess beads. Place these extra beads back in their container. Repeat with the silver metallic Beedz.

7. Add a few dots of silver dimensional paint where you want a little extra sparkle. Press small rhinestones in the center of each dot. The paint works as a glue and forms a little rim around the "gem" like a bezel.

8. Glue the baked cane edge pieces just inside the outer edges to form a border.

The side of the box.

9. When the front is completely dry, glue baked cane slices of your choice along the sides and on the top. Add silver dimensional paint curlicues to complement the cane slices.

The back of the box.

10. For the back of the box, draw curlicue lines with the silver dimensional paint and add a few decorative elements to coordinate with the front. Keep the back design simpler to minimize damage to the box decor when it is opened and in use.

11. Place a stick-on magnet on the inside of the lid. Use this to hold metal cutting blades in place and safely in view so you won't have to dig around for a blade (see page 17).

Fill the box with customized tools. It's easy to cover the handle of an X-acto knife, bead reamer, and other etching and carving tools with polymer clay. Use scrap clay to form handles that fit your grip perfectly.

Cover the lid of a candy mint box or other small metal box with matching or coordinating clay and use it to hold a ponce bag with powder and a small brush for use with molds and textures. Cover more of them and use to keep small tools such as Kemper cutters.

Grandparents' Day:
Memory Box for Playing Cards

Card box top.

My mother heard the story of a woman who paid creative tribute to her mother with a collection of teacups. On the underside of each teacup she placed a printed strip of paper that told something about her mother, who had loved pretty teacups and always turned them over to examine the bottom for trademarks and so on.

My mother took this idea in another direction (because creativity is catching!). Her mother was a schoolteacher and an artist, but also a dedicated card player. She played cards just about every day of her life once she was old enough to hold and count them. She always preferred pretty decks, not just plain cards, so it was only natural that instead of teacups for a memento, my mother chose playing cards! She wrote 52 remembrances – two or three sentences each – to go on 52 playing cards, which I designed and printed with my computer.

Approximate Size:

4-1/4" x 3"

You will need

box
decorative card to match or coordinate with the playing cards
1/2 oz. ivory clay
stamps, texture items
Aztec Gold PearlEx powder
white glue
Flecto Varathane

Decorating the box

Note: *The box I chose had nice gold and black sides already, but if* *yours doesn't, you can paint it and allow it to dry before decorating.*

1. Brush a small amount of white glue on the lid. Press the decorative card firmly in place, removing air bubbles as needed. Remove any glue that seeps out at the edges. Allow to dry.

2. Use a soft-bristle brush to apply a thin coat of varathane (I used satin finish) over the card. Allow the varathane to dry.

3. Roll out a 5" long strip of ivory clay at the #3 setting or by hand to a thickness of 1/16".

4. Impress the strip with texture using rubber stamps or other items.

5. Apply gold PearlEx powder to the raised portions of the clay.

6. Cut two strips the length of the box top. Trim to just cover the outside edge of the card and to extend to the edges of the box. Cut small triangles or other shapes from the textured clay to fit between the strips and cover much of the exposed top and bottom edges of the cards.

7. Bake according to the clay package directions.

8. Apply a coat of varathane to protect the powders. When the varathane is dry, glue the pieces on the box.

This embellishment totally changed the look of the box. And it now matches the playing cards I designed, making it part of a set. Personal projects like these are great to do in your own family style!

SUMMER GALLERY

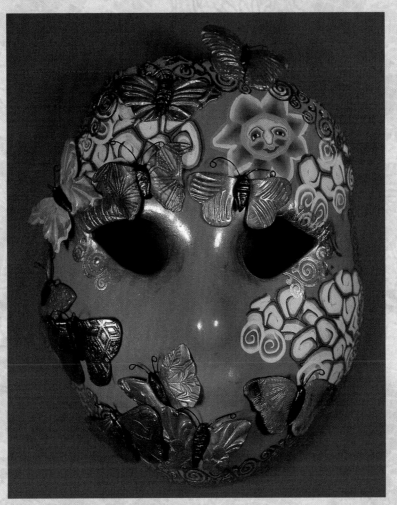

Sarajane Helm. "Summer Mask."

Ann Raymond. Two views of "Last Dance."

Photos by Janis Carpenter.

Janet Scheetz. "At the Beach" thong necklace and earrings.

Deborah and Marah Anderson. "Sandals."

Kathleen Bolan. "Summer Solstice."

Leigh Ross. Gold leaf and cobalt blue vessels.

 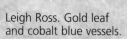

Kathy Weaver. "Patriotic Purse."

Photo by Snapshots.

Sarajane Helm. "Miss Firecracker."

Photo by Florence Maio.

Sylvia Schmahmann. "Patriotic Pin."

Tamila Darling and Layl McDill. Red, white, and blue summertime canes.

Sarajane Helm. "Summer's Breeze" necklace and earring set.

Judith Skinner. "Summer Silk" necklace.

Olga Porteous. "Guatemalan Rainbow" necklace.

Kathleen Bolan. "Somewhere Over the...Edge."

Photo by Jerry Anthony.

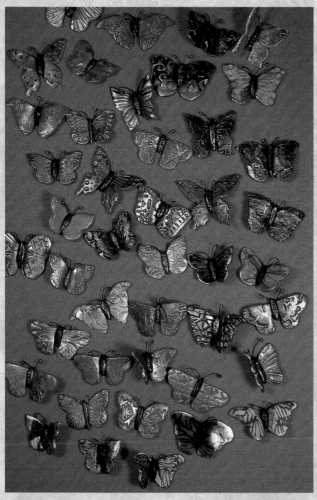

Sarajane Helm. "Butterflies."

Leigh Ross. "Capt. Tripps" candleholder.

Marie Segal. "Green Man" pin.

Robin Williams. "Graduation Pin."

Sarajane Helm. Face pendant and butterflies.

Sarajane Helm. "A Nod to Miss Miranda" face pins.

Donna Kato. "Butterfly Frame and Face Cane" made of Kato Polyclay.

Leigh Ross. "Millennium Garden" canes applied to ceramic tile.

Dawn Naylor. "Happy Birthday to Me" polymer clay, paper, and string.

Sarajane Helm. "Full Blown Rose of Summer."

PROJECTS FOR AUTUMN

"Listen! The wind is rising,
and the air is wild with leaves,
We have had our summer evenings,
now for October eves."

-Autumn, Humbert Wolfe

AUTUMN BRINGS THE WINDS AND BLOWS IN THE

time of drastic changes. Temperatures begin to fall, as do the leaves; some people name the entire season Fall! But before the leaves drop down, they put on the most astounding display of rich dramatic color variations. Autumn is an incredibly busy time as nature sends out the signal that the cold times are soon coming...and the wealth of foods and natural materials are ready for the final harvest.

All the living creatures of the world share an urge to store up the treasures that a fruitful growing season has provided, even though our lives may not be as directly tied to the land cycles as once they were. We all feel the tides change toward days that are becoming shorter and nights much colder, and we take a moment or two to appreciate and reflect on all that we have now, in this time of plenty, facing the darker days that surely come, and the brighter ones again after that. It is the cold of advancing autumn that makes the pumpkins sweeter. The signs all around proclaim that summer is losing its fiery grip and winter awaits, just out of sight. It reminds us all of how sweet and full the last of the warm times can be in our year and in life itself.

"Autumn Collage" features cane slices by Sarajane Helm, Leigh Ross, Dawn Naylor, Donna Kato, Nancy Osbahr, Janet Scheetz, Tamila Darling, Stefanie Wagner, Mary-Lu Elliot, Ellen Berne, Candace Mathewson, Marie Segal, and Jan VanDonkelaar.

Autumnal Equinox:
Leaf Pins

"Falling Leaves" is the name of a song, and it's also a strong visual image. Autumn leaves can be made using polymer clay and PearlEx powders. You can cut them out using leaf cutters or cut around a real leaf to create a clay replica.

Approximate size:

2" to 3"

You will need

1 oz. each of polymer clays in autumn colors – gold, brown, red, purple, orange
leaf cutters or paper pattern
stamps or texture plates
PearlEx powders or Fimo Bronzepulvers in autumn colors – copper, gold, purple, red
bead reamer or needle tool
Flecto Varathane

Making the leaves

1. Choose a few colors of clay and roll them together through a pasta roller set at #3 or #4 or by hand to a thickness of 1/16". The colors can be blotchy or distributed like watercolors. The more times you fold and pass the sheet through the pasta roller, the more blended the colors will become.

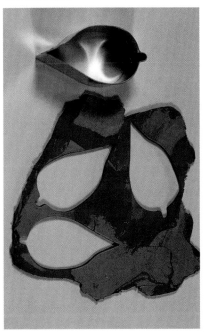

Cut leaves from a blended clay sheet.

2. Use leaf-shaped cutters to cut out leaves or cut around a leaf or leaf pattern with a knife.

Left: The clay cutout. Middle: After pressing the clay into a stamp. Right: After applying powder.

3. Press the cutout leaves into a stamp or texture plate to make a raised pattern if you like.

4. To create veins, use the back of a knife or a skewer tip to score lines in the leaves down the center and radiating from the center to the leaf tips.

5. Apply PearlEx powder or Fimo Bronzepulver highlights on the raised areas. Apply powder along the outside edges if desired. Bend the leaf slightly to make it look more natural.

6. Use a needle or bead reamer to make a hole in the stem area of the leaf if you want to hang it later.

7. Bake according to the clay package directions for 30 minutes, then coat all the powdered pieces with varathane.

These leaves can be made into earrings, pins, or strung into necklaces. They can also be used to decorate household items or as part of an interesting display.

Back to School:
Star Students

This is a great group project for teachers, scout leaders, or parents. All you need is a star-shaped cookie cutter, some clay, and a Polaroid or 35mm print picture of each student. For larger groups and younger children, or if time is limited, start with preconditioned sheets of clay or use cut out clay shapes all ready to go.

Have students wash their hands carefully before and after all clay projects. Take along a box of premoistened wipes to start the cleaning process, then have them wash with soap and water. Polymer clay is nontoxic but hands should be washed after using any art supply.

Have an adult supervise or do all baking, and follow the directions on the package.

Approximate Size:

3"

You will need

Note: *These amounts are for a group. Less than 1 oz. is used for each star.*

1 lb. Premo gold clay
1 lb. blue clay
star-shaped cutter, larger than the photos (mine is 2-1/2 " across)
toothpicks
gold thread for hanging stars
photo of each child, trimmed to fit inside the star
permanent felt tip pen
1/4 piece of paper for each student
glitter (optional)

Making the star

1. Roll the clay through a pasta roller at the #3 setting or by hand to a thickness of 1/16". Cut out as many stars as needed.

2. Give a clay star and a 1/4 sheet of paper to each student, along with a toothpick and a small chunk of clay (about 1/4 oz.). Have each student write their name on the paper (to keep the pieces identified during the baking process). Place the clay star on the paper.

3. Show students how to roll snakes and balls of clay and have them use these pieces to secure the edges of their photo to the clay star. Have them use the toothpick to poke a hanging hole in the clay star and to carve designs in the clay if desired

4. Sprinkle with glitter if desired. Collect the stars and bake them according to the clay package directions. Collect any remaining clay and pass out premoistened wipes for hand cleaning.

5. After baking, have the students sign and date the back of their ornament using a permanent felt tip pen. If the students are too young, have an adult do the writing

These can be turned into magnets (glue a magnet in place on the back) or done as ornaments with a thread hanger. Or use with a pushpin to decorate a bulletin board. These can be taped in place on displays, and even sewn or glued to banners.

Star ornaments are easy to make. Any shaped cookie cutter can be used to make very easy ornaments when you start with a sheet of patterned clay. Even a solid color such as red with some gold leaf added and stretched during the rollout can be very beautiful. Stars and flat ornaments can be affixed to the front of a card or sent along with it inside, and mailed at little or no extra cost.

Projects for Autumn ❧ **103**

Halloween:
Miniature Tribal Mask

The line between the cycles of the living and the dead becomes more and more apparent in the autumn. It's no coincidence that the Mexican Day of the Dead, Halloween, and All Soul's Day all focus on the importance of the passage from one plane of existence to another, and remind us that dying is a part of the continuing cycle.

Approximate Size:

3"

You will need

2 oz. block of Premo cadmium red
pea-sized piece of Premo black
Gold PearlEx powder or Fimo
    Bronzepulver
cardboard tube
mask stamp (I used New Zealand Mask
    #31083 from Uptown Design)
needle tool or bead reamer
triangular cutter (from the large
    aspic set)
star-shaped cookie cutter with fluted
    edge
Flecto Varathane
dark stain (recipe on page 25)
1200-grit wet/dry sandpaper

Making the mask

1. Mix the red clay with enough black to "sadden" the tone and make it look more aged, or more like red lacquer or cinnabar. How much is a matter of choice.

2. Roll the mixed and conditioned clay through a pasta roller set at #3 or by hand to a thickness of 1/16".

Press the clay sheet onto a stamp.

3. Press the clay sheet onto a lightly powdered stamp (use a ponce bag to apply powder), being careful to press the clay down in every part and

over the edges of the design. Carefully use an acrylic roller or brayer to further press the clay into the stamp. Peel the clay away from the stamp and lay it flat on your work surface.

Cut a triangle from the top center.

4. Use a triangular cutter to remove clay in the top center, using the top of the "nose" portion of the design as a guide. This removal forms the horns of this mask.

Flute the edges.

5. Use a knife to cut away clay 1/16" or so from the edge of the design on the sides of the mask. Stop across from the whorls and use the edge of the fluted cookie cutter to finish trimming the mask away from the rest of the clay. Use the cutter in three steps, starting at the bottom level and going up. Repeat on the other side and across the bottom of the mask for jagged edges.

6. Use your fingertip to smooth each indentation and all the edges of the mask.

7. With the blade of the knife, lightly score lines all around the sides and bottom edge of the mask.

Poke eyeholes.

8. Use a needle tool to poke eyeholes at the center of each whorl.

Add gold powder at the eye whorls. The right side of the mask shows the black stain applied and wiped off.

9. With your fingertip, add a small amount of gold powder to the raised areas of the eye whorls.

10. Bend the mask slightly to round the form. Place it over a cardboard tube and bake in a preheated oven at 270°F or according to package instructions for 30 minutes.

11. When cool, sand carefully to remove any gold powder that is not centered on the whorls.

12. Use a paintbrush to apply a small amount of varathane over the gold powdered area only. Allow to dry.

13. Use a plastic bristle paintbrush to apply the dark stain mixture to the mask, making sure to get it into the impressed areas. Apply the stain all over the mask, then use a rag to wipe it from all the raised areas of the mask, leaving it only in the recesses. Repeat if there are any areas that need a little more (it's easy to wipe away too much). Check to make sure you didn't miss any spots.

14. Allow the mask to dry for several hours, then gently rub the wet/dry sandpaper over the mask several times to remove any paint residue from the raised surface. This brings out the difference between the top and shadowed areas.

15. Add a leather loop or pin back if desired.

portion of the design on a large stamp). Press the clay firmly into the stamp.

3. Lay the clay sheet flat on your work surface and cut a 2" rectangle. Shape it so the bottom is slightly narrower than the top. Smooth the edges with your fingertip.

4. Press the bottom edge of the rectangle into the smallest size bumps on a grater. Place the mask back down on your work surface.

5. Using the larger teardrop cutter, cut two eyepieces from scraps of rolled out black clay. Position the eyepieces on the mask and press them lightly in place.

6. Center the smaller teardrop cutter in the eyepieces to cut eyeholes, leaving oval rims around the holes.

7. Center the square cutter below the eyes and cut out the mouth area.

8. Using your fingertip, lightly apply gold powder to the raised areas of the mask.

9. Place the mask on a toilet paper roll and curve it around the roll.

10. Bake the paper roll and mask for 30 minutes according to package directions. Allow to cool.

11. Apply a coat of varathane to protect the powder.

To use the mask as a pendant, place a dot of glue 1/4" from the mask top and firmly press the bottom end of a thin leather strip into it. Be careful not to use so much glue that you get excess on your fingers. Allow the leather and clay to bond, then place another dot of glue just below the leather strip, bend the strip back to form a loop, and firmly press the end into the glue. Allow the glue to dry before threading the mask onto a cord, ribbon, or strands of beads.

For a pin, after baking press a small wad of black clay on the back of the mask to form a flat surface. Use liquid polymer clay to glue on a pin back and rebake at the directed temperature for another 30 minutes.

Approximate Size:

2"

You will need

1 oz. Premo black clay
Gold PearlEx powder
rubber stamp (I used the Large Faux Bird Post from Uptown Design Co.)
grater
2 teardrop-shaped cutters, 3/8" and 1/2"
square Kemper cutter, 3/8"
cardboard toilet paper roll
Flecto Varathane

Making the mask

1. Roll well conditioned clay through a pasta roller at the #3 setting or by hand to a thickness of 1/16".

2. Lightly powder the corner of the rubber stamp (you'll only use a

Use just the corner of this Uptown Design Co. stamp to impress the design.

Veterans Day:
Poppy Memory Box

I keep my grandfather's letters and postcards in this box. There is also room for his dog tags and my Granny's glasses, making a little treasure trove of reminders of them both. Think about the people and their interests when you create your own memory boxes. These boxes can be a conduit to forgotten stories that other family members will recall and share with you.

Going through old family photographs is a way of connecting with our heritage in different times and places. Our stories take place within the context of matters on a much wider scale, whether we know it at the time or not, and familiar threads become part of the larger tapestry. When postcards and letters are saved and cherished, eventually they become historical. Protected storage in a sturdy box is critical for fragile items such as papers or letters. Any box can be decorated to make it more special and so that it becomes part of the presentation of the collection as well.

My grandfather wrote letters home when he was still a very young man, long ago and far away and missing those he loved. He was in his teens and early 20s, fighting in World War I, and these letters came from France and other parts of Europe where he was stationed. These treasured letters are still here, and though the ink has faded, they stand as potent reminders.

We change in our lives, and change again – going from babies to children who become adults, then middle-aged, then older still, and then gone, changed to something else again and leaving only reminders. Some can be held in the hand as well as the heart!

My grandfather was much affected by his experiences in the war. The person he was when he sent letters home formed the person I knew and loved nearly half a century later. He felt very deeply about the poem "In Flander's Fields" by Major John Mcree, and said that it stated enough about the war. He himself didn't want to say anything more about it, so I used the first verse of this once popular poem in decorating the lid of the letterbox.

Approximate Size:

5-1/2" x 8" x 2-1/2"

You will need

plain box to decorate
decorative paper
printed poem if desired
variety of embellishments (cane slices, buttons, clay tiles)
Flecto Varathane, satin finish
Sobo craft glue
Super Glue

Decorating the box

1. Find a box that will suit your purpose. I chose an empty tin box with a shoe polish ad on the top.

2. Assemble a variety of embellishments. I used polymer clay tiles, antique buttons, and lace cane slices. Tailor your selection to include items or symbols that are significant or pleasing. Choose decorative paper to serve as a background and cut it to fit on the lid, leaving enough room for a narrow metal border.

3. Affix the decorative paper to the top of the lid with Sobo craft glue. Use a brayer to remove any wrinkles. I added a printed poem on top of the decorative paper.

4. Apply a coat of varathane over the papers.

5. Super Glue the embellishments to the lid, covering any raw edges of the paper. Use craft glue to affix the pieces to the paper.

"In Flander's fields the poppies blow, between the crosses row on row." These first lines of the poem hit home to many people in that era. Because of Mcree's poem, poppies came to symbolize the Veterans of Foreign Wars, an enduring reminder that's still in use today. My grandfather grew flame-red poppies behind his house. They remind me of him even without the other connotation, so the poppies I used to decorate this box work doubly well.

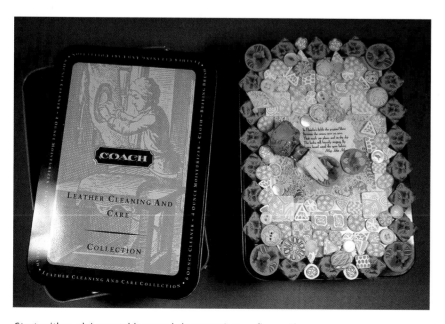

Start with a plain metal box and decorate it to reflect a theme.

AUTUMN GALLERY

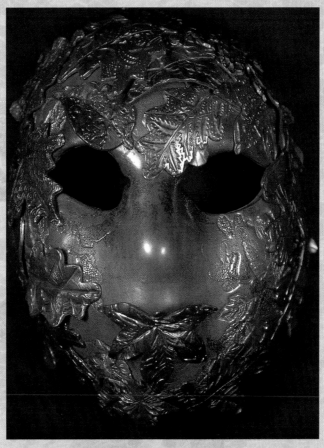

Sarajane Helm. "Autumn Mask."

Dawn Naylor. "Autumn Leaves."

Sarajane Helm. "Leaf Face" pendant.

Marie Segal. "Two Vessels."

Leigh Ross used real leaves as templates in cutting and forming all the leaves in this wreath.

Judith Skinner. "Unfallen Leaves" necklace and back detail. This piece won a prize at Embellishments. Notice the precise workmanship and attention to detail in the stringing technique.

Joanne Banuelos. "Dia de los Muertos Skulls 2."

Marie Segal. "Green Men in Autumn" pins.

Joanne Banuelos. "Devilish Beauty."

Joanne Banuelos. "Lovely Muerto."

Photo by SnapShots.

Kathy Weaver. "Fall Necklace."

Photo by Barbara Hunt.

Ellen Berne. "Autumnal Pod Necklace."

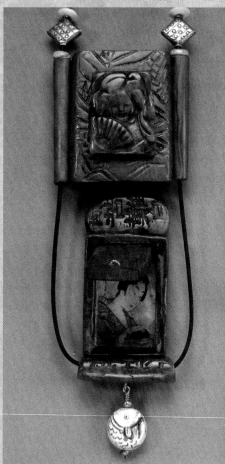

Jean Cohen. "Wise Woman" Croning
Celebration necklace and detail.

Photos by Norman Watkins.

Sarajane Helm. "Ready for Halloween."

Sarajane Helm. "Fortunes Told."

From the Internet Miniature Masks Swap 2002, Set 3. From the top left, these were made by: Rose Mary Martin, Bill Girard, Lori Greenberg, Sherry Bailey, Sherry Bailey, Julie Leir-Van Sickle, Collen "Sunni" Bergeron, Karen Omodt, Jen Santoro, Sarajane Helm, Ellen Knaeur, Sherry Bailey, Judy Jussaud, Sarajane Helm, Karen Omodt, Lisa Carlson, Denita Johnson, Denise Standifer, Helen Hughes, Tonja Lenderman, LynnDel Newbold, Barbara Hart, Cecelia Shepherd, Rose Mary Martin, Ellen Knauer, and BrendaLea Abbott.

Ian Helm. "Miniature Monster Masks."

Ian and Andy Helm.
Glow-in-the-dark ghost pins.

Tamila Darling.
"Black Cat Pin and Pumpkin Bracelet."

Halloween canes by Janet Scheetz, Layl McDill, Stefanie Wagner, Mary-Lu Elliot, and Candace Mathewson.

Photo by SnapShots.

Tamila Darling. "Trick or Treat."

Leigh Ross. A seasonal lunchbox and detail shows the precision Leigh builds into her canes.

Projects for Winter

"The north wind doth blow, and we shall have snow,
And what will poor Robin do then, poor thing?
He'll sit in a barn to keep himself warm,
And hide his head under his wing, poor thing!"

—Nursery rhyme, Anonymous

WINTER BRINGS TOGETHER THE BEGINNING AND

end of the yearly cycle. That's why two-faced Janus, who saw the future and the past together, became the namesake of January, the first full month of winter. The days are short and cold, cold, cold. The nights are long and dark and even colder! And yet there is great beauty to be found outdoors in spite of the conditions that keep most living things in check or dormant, waiting for balmier times.

Purple and blue shadows in the snow, the delicate tracery of bare tree limbs or ice-coated hedges show exquisite detail and a wealth of subtle color and intricate form. Snowflakes themselves are infinitely varied, even in a blizzard.

The contrast of the weather and the warmth of the fire indoors is a powerful incentive for gatherings and parties, generating shared body heat and camaraderie both. With less work to do outside, there has traditionally been more time for handcrafts and beautification during the hours of winter, combined with a need for keeping hands and minds occupied and focused. Parties for shared work and just for fun bring warmth to cold times, and make us aware that we aren't alone in the world. It's no accident that many holidays and celebrations held at this time of year use candles and fire as part of the symbolic show. It is a time when both sides of things show – light and dark, fire and ice, and air so crisp and quiet that you can hear carolers at Christmas singing or church bells ringing from far away.

"Winter Collage" features cane slices by Sarajane Helm, Leigh Ross, Nancy Osbahr, Z Kripke, Carol L. Simmons, Janet Scheetz, Tamila Darling, Judy Belcher, Linda Hess, Stefanie Wagner, Mary-Lu Elliot, Ellen Berne, Candace Mathewson, and Jan VanDonkelaar.

Winter Solstice:
Snowflakes

Sarajane Helm. Snowflakes.

Dawn Naylor. Snowflakes.

These snowflakes can be amazingly simple to make with white or pearlized clay and a topping of glitter. For more intricate snowflakes, cut the shapes out of a sheet of cane-patterned clay. There are lots of snowflake cookie cutters available on the market. Off The Beaten Path (see Sources, page 143) offers a nesting set of three different sized cutters and two pointy-shaped cutters for removing inside sections from the snowflakes.

Dawn Naylor and I each used the same cutter set, with beautifully different results – hers are made with icy cool tones of blues and purples along with white and translucent, and I did a set with white, ivory, and translucent.

Approximate Size:

1" to 5"

You will need

2 oz. white or pearlized clay
cane slices for decorations (optional)
glitter
snowflake cutters or six-pointed star cutters
small round or teardrop cutters

Making the snowflakes

1. Roll conditioned clay through a pasta roller at the #4 setting or by hand to a thickness of 1/20". You can go even thinner with practice, but this is a good overall thickness.

2. If desired, cut thin slices of your favorite canes and affix them to the clay sheet, then reroll it through the pasta roller or by hand to meld the cane slices completely into the clay sheet.

Start with larger cutters, then use smaller ones to cut out middles.

3. Press the largest snowflake cutter into the clay sheet first. Hold the cutter in place and pull the excess clay from around it.

4. Position one of the small cutters inside the snowflake cutout and carefully remove the inner snowflake. This not only forms the inside of the large flake, it makes another one too!

5. Use your fingertip to carefully stroke all exposed edges to smooth any rough spots.

6. Place the snowflake on a piece of cardstock or paper for baking so you don't have to pick it up again (this becomes difficult with the delicate and lacy snowflake).

Cut out small sections to create a lacy effect.

7. With the smaller pointed cutters, remove portions of the snowflake to shape it to your liking.

8. Apply glitter as desired by shaking it on the raw snowflakes – it will stay in place after baking. You can make an entire batch of snowflakes, then give them a shake of glitter. I love the holographic and crystal glitters available now, but gold or silver can also be very effective.

9. Bake at 260° for 30 minutes.

You can use a six-pointed star cutter to make snowflakes.

If using a six-pointed star cutter, cut out several pieces and use one of the points or a smaller cutter to cut notches in the inside angle of all six points as shown. Use it again to cut notches halfway between the first notches you cut and the points of the stars. Use a pointed stick, straw, or small Kemper tools to remove small interior portions if desired.

You can also decorate snowflakes by impressing the unbaked cutouts into a texture sheet or rubber stamp, or use the stamps with metallic or colored inks and apply to the raw clay.

Poke a hole in the more solid flakes to hang them (snowflakes with cutout sections don't require a hole for hanging, just use a hole that's already there). Hang them by tying a length of white thread through the poked holes or cut sections.

You can also glue earring backs to small snowflakes for instant Snow Day accessories! A few of them placed on the tablecloth make for quick and easy winter decor, or glue them to a card for an invitation to a Winter Solstice, Christmas, or Hanukah party.

Cabin Fever:
Party Invitation

Approximate Size:

5-1/4" x 8-1/2"

You will need

baked polymer clay snowflakes
computer/printer or pen and ink
white cardstock and envelopes
rubber stamp (I used Blizzard
   #115271 from Uptown Design)
stamp inkpads
glitter
decorative-edge scissors
white glue

Making the invitation

1. Use your computer or pen and ink to create a message. I used "You Are Invited." Get as fancy as you like. Colored cardstock shows off white snowflakes very well.

2. Fold the cardstock in half. Cut the bottom edge with decorative scissors.

3. Use the stamp and ink pads to decorate the face of the card and the edge of the envelope. I used blue ink and metallic gold to build up an interesting composition.

4. Apply small spots of white glue at random, then pour glitter on the card. Do this over newspaper to minimize the mess. Tap the card to re-

Stamp designs on the cardstock and envelope.

move excess glitter. Return the excess to the container or dispose of it in the wastebasket.

5. Apply white glue to the backs of the polymer snowflakes and press them on the card. Allow to dry overnight before mailing.

Hanukah:
Covered Candleholder

To make a Hanukah Menorah, make nine decorated candleholders. Glue one to a base to raise it higher than the others. Paint the base to match or cover it with polymer too. This taller candle is called the "Shammes" and is used to light the other candles in the traditional Judaic Festival of the Lights.

Approximate Size:

2"

You will need

unfinished wood candle cups
square canes of snowflake designs
(see page 31 for making instructions)
blue acrylic paint
Interference Blue PearlEx powder
Flecto Varathane
white glue

Covering the candleholder

1. Mix a small amount of varathane with blue acrylic paint. Use the varathane instead of water to thin the paint, and add enough to get a creamy workable mixture. Add a small amount (less than 1/4 tea-spoon) of PearlEx powder to give it a wonderful sheen. Mix thoroughly.

2. Paint the top rim of the wood cup, extending down slightly onto the body. Apply several coats, allow-ing each coat to dry before applying the next one. You do not need to paint the inside of the cup.

3. After the last coat dries, apply a thin even coat of white glue on the exposed wood. You can wait until this dries or apply the clay while it is still tacky. Even when the glue is dry, it creates a bond between the raw clay and the wood.

4. Slice even pieces of a polymer clay cane. Press them in place around the body of the candle cup. This may

Place square cane slices around the cup.

take two or three slices per candle cup. Line them up evenly, cut off the excess or stretch the slices slightly to fit if needed. Smooth the seams together with your fingertip.

5. Bake the candle cups accord-ing to package directions.

You can also use these candle cups on top of taller spindles of turned wood or other items. Paint these to match and glue or screw the cups firmly into place before using. Remember to never leave candles burning unattended.

Christmas:
Faux Gingerbread Ornament

Ian and Andy Helm. Faux gingerbread ornaments.

Approximate Size:

3-1/2"

You will need

2 oz. each of Premo white and burnt sienna clay (this will make several ornaments)
gingerbread man (or bear) cookie cutter
Kemper star cutter
8" gold thread (per ornament)
white glue
paper
toothpick

Making the ornament

1. Roll the conditioned sienna clay through a pasta roller at the #3 setting or by hand to a thickness of 1/16".

2. Place the gingerbread man cutter on the sheet and press. Tear the excess clay away from the cutter edges.

3. Release the ornament from the work surface by sliding a knife under it. Use your fingertip to smooth the outside edges.

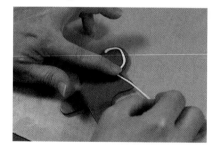

Decorate the gingerbread man with "icing."

4. Roll the white clay into a long thin snake. Use it like icing to decorate the gingerbread person. This can be done in many ways – as an outline all around, outlined clothes, etc.

Add details.

5. Roll out small balls of white clay and use them for eyes, buttons, hair, and other details. Use a toothpick to indent holes in the buttons or to mark other details as desired. These can be fancy or simple, and all are fun to do!

6. Carefully turn over the decorated ornament and place a spot of white glue on the back of the head. Fold the gold thread and place the ends in the glue to form a loop for hanging.

7. Use the star cutter to cut a small brown star out of the brown clay sheet scraps. Glue the star on top of the thread ends. Gently press it in place, being careful not to mar the decorations. The glue will help hold the thread and star.

8. Turn the ornament face up again and place it on a piece of paper, then on a baking sheet.

9. Bake according to the clay package directions for 30 minutes.

Christmas:
Tree Ornament

Bobby

Approximate Size:

3-1/2"

You will need

2 oz. each of Premo sap green and
  sienna clay (this will make several
  ornaments)
small amounts of red, blue, yellow,
  and white clay
Christmas tree cookie cutter
paper
Kemper star cutter
8" gold thread (per ornament)
white glue
opalescent glitter
gold Beedz or glitter (if desired)

Making the ornament

1. Separately roll the conditioned green and brown clay through a pasta roller at the #3 setting or by hand to a thickness of 1/16".

Position the cutter on the joined strips.

2. Cut both colors into strips. The green strip is for the foliage and must be at least twice as wide as the brown, which is for the trunk. Butt the two strips together with the brown below the green, press with your finger to seal the seam, and flatten.

3. Place the tree cookie cutter so the green fills the tree section and the brown fills the trunk section. Cut the ornament out of the clay, tearing the excess clay away from the cutter. Use your fingertip to smooth the raw edges.

Add garland and ornaments.

4. Roll the white clay into a long thin snake. Apply it like a garland, in loops or zigzags as desired.

5. Roll tiny balls of the other colored clays and use to decorate the tree.

Twist red and white snakes.

6. Roll out small thin snakes of red and white. Twist them together and cut into 1" sections. Bend these at the top to form candy canes and place them on the tree.

7. Flatten a bit of yellow clay and punch out a small star using the Kemper cutter. If desired, press the front of the star into some gold Beedz or glitter before applying it. Press the star into place at the top of the tree.

Score lines in the trunk.

8. Use a knife blade or toothpick to score lines in the tree trunk to give it a bark-like texture.

9. Carefully turn over the ornament. Place a spot of white glue on the back of the tree at the top. Fold the gold thread and place the ends in the glue to form a loop for hanging.

10. Use the Kemper cutter to cut a green or red star out of leftover clay and glue the star on top of the thread ends. Gently press it in place, being careful not to mar the decorations. The glue will help hold the thread and star.

11. Turn the ornament face up, place it on a piece of paper, then on a baking sheet.

12. Bake according to package directions for 30 minutes.

Change the look by using different embellishments.

Christmas:
Angel Pin

Wear your angel pin on a jacket or hatband, or attach it to a ribbon or bow as part of a wreath or larger decorative piece. Make several to give as gifts before the holidays. Your friends will love having an angel to watch over them.

You can use face canes to make all sorts of pins or ornaments – an angel, a dancehall girl with gaudy earrings and a feather in her hair, a sweet little girl, or a saucy lady. Glue on a pin back or attach a gold thread loop hanger to use as an ornament.

Approximate Size:

3"

You will need

face cane (see page 40 for making
    instructions)
hair cane (see page 45 for making
    instructions)
wing cane (see page 45 for making
    instructions)
lace cane for dress if desired (see
    page 32 for making instructions)
2 oz. Premo white or pearl clay for
    backing
1 oz. Premo gold clay
gold leaf
Flecto Varathane
pin back
Super Glue

Making the pin

1. Roll the white or pearl clay through a pasta roller at the #4 setting or by hand to a thickness of 1/20". This will be the backing for the piece. You could use scrap clay, but if you use translucent lace canes for the dress, the backing will show through.

2. Cut a thin slice of the face cane and place it on the backing clay, but don't press it into the backing yet.

3. Cut two wing slices and place them on either side of the face, slightly away from and below it. This leaves room for the hair. Don't press these pieces into the backing yet.

Add hair cane pieces to the face and wing slices on the background.

4. Cut hair cane pieces and place them as desired. I often bring one curl down over a shoulder. Don't

press these in yet – you may need to reposition pieces.

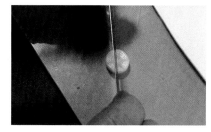

Cut lace cane slices in half for the dress bodice.

5. Cut white and translucent (lace) cane slices to use as the dress bodice. I used a white and translucent snowflake cane for this example. Cut these slices in half and place them under the face and over to the wings. Lift up the hair as needed and place the lace cane underneath it.

Roll with an acrylic rod to meld the pieces together.

6. Press all canes in place with your fingers, then use an acrylic rod to roll over the assemblage until all the canes are smoothly affixed and melded together.

7. Roll the gold clay through a pasta roller at the #5 setting or by hand to a thickness of 1/24".

Place gold clay on gold leaf.

8. Place the gold clay sheet on the gold leaf. It is easier to place the clay on the leaf than it is to place the leaf on the clay. Burnish the leaf on the clay with your fingertip.

Place the halo in the angel's hair.

9. Use a craft knife to cut a small thin strip of the gold for a halo. Curve it with your fingers and place it on the angel's hair.

10. Add any other details such as a flower on the bodice or earrings. Springtime angels can also have flowers in their hair! Use the roller to again flatten all components together.

Cut around the angel to remove it from the backing.

11. Holding a craft knife like a pencil, cut around the angel to remove it from the backing. Lightly press the edges down toward the table to round them off a bit and give a more finished edge to the piece. Smooth the entire piece with your fingertip to remove any fingerprints.

12. Place the piece in a baking pan and bake according to the clay package directions for 30 minutes.

13. After the piece cools, apply a small amount of varathane on the gold leaf to protect it.

14. Super Glue a pin back to the back of the angel. Always place pin backs in the top half of a piece so it won't tip forward when worn.

As a variation, use pearlized colored clays instead of cane slices for the dress bodice. Leave them plain or decorate them with gold or silver designs, using a favorite rubber stamp and inkpad or PearlEx powders.

Christmas:
Cute Critter Ornaments

I have been making variations of these little critters for many years, and they always get a warm response when people see them. They can be used to make jewelry, hanging ornaments, or decorations on packages. They also look great glued on other decorative items such as boxes and candleholders. Or put several on a wreath or floral arrangement. They are wonderful in a child's room around the base of a lamp or to beautify a wooden peg hanger. Try a few on the corners of a frame or added to a mirror or whatnot shelf. They can be made for Christmas, but also for birthdays, and anytime!

All the critters start with the same body type – a teardrop-shaped piece of clay made by rolling a ball and pointing one end slightly. Changing details such as ears, nose, legs, wings, or horns all add up to a different cute critter.

Shown here are the directions for a reindeer, pig, and bird. With a few variations you can make all kinds of critters – sheep, mice, elephants, bears, cats, dogs, and more!

Approximate Size:

1-1/4" to 2-1/4"

You will need

small amounts of clay – brown,
  pink, red, yellow, blue, green,
  white/ivory, black
gold thread

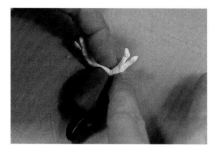

1. Roll a teardrop-shaped piece of brown clay for the head and body.

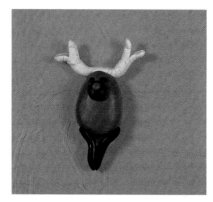

Roll a thin black snake for the legs.

2. Roll out a thin black snake for the legs. Cut the snake in two pieces, each about as long as the body.

Press the legs into the body.

3. Lightly press the legs together along the bottom, and splay the tops apart to form a Y shape. Press the legs in place at the bottom of the body.

Slice apart for 1/4 " on each end.

4. Roll a thicker snake of white/ivory clay for the antlers. Twist the snake slightly to give it a little texture. Use the blade of a knife to slice both ends of the antler piece about 1/4 " from each end.

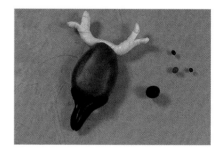

Press the antlers onto the head.

5. Spread these apart slightly to form the branches of the antlers and twist the cut ends slightly to round the sections off a bit. You may need to use a toothpick to press the center of the antlers on the top of the head and shape to form the antlers.

6. Roll a pea-sized ball of black clay to form the reindeer's muzzle. Place it on the face section, just slightly below the antlers. You want a bit of the brown to show all around the muzzle, so don't connect it to the antlers.

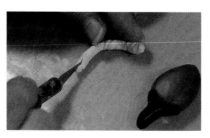

Roll balls for the muzzle, eyes, and nose.

7. Roll a small red ball for the nose and place it in the center of the muzzle.

8. Roll two very small balls for eyes (or use tiny black seed beads). Place the eyes a small distance apart just above the muzzle.

9. Bake in a preheated oven according to package directions for 30 minutes.

1. Roll a teardrop-shaped piece of pink clay to form the head and body.

Use a toothpick to impress lines on the snout.

2. Roll a small ball of pink clay for the snout and place it on the teardrop in the face area, slightly down from the top. Use a toothpick to add two impressed lines for nostrils in the snout.

Bend the ear pieces and press them in place.

3. Roll two more pink balls about the same size and flatten them into ovals for the ears. Bend them slightly in the center and press one end of each into the top of the head.

Slit to form a cloven hoof.

4. Roll two black balls for the trotters (pig feet). Flatten them slightly against your fingertip and use a craft knife to slit each trotter about halfway up. Open the cuts to form the cloven hooves and press them in place at the bottom of the pig body.

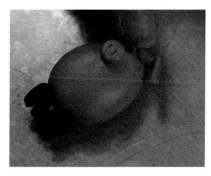

Place tiny black eyes.

5. Roll two tiny black balls for eyes and place them above the snout.

Note: *To make this a Christmas pig, add holly leaves and berries to the head of the pig. You can skip this step completely or add other decorative bits instead such as flowers, a cowboy hat, wings for a flying pig – whatever you like!*

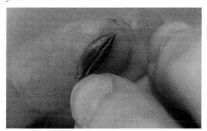

Score down the center with your fingernail.

6. Make the holly leaf by rolling a small ball of green clay and flattening it between your finger and thumb. Point both ends in a leaf shape and score down the center length with your fingernail. Poke with your fingernail at about the halfway point and bend the green piece in half to form two leaves. Apply this to the pig's head, using a toothpick to nudge it firmly in place.

Press holly berries on the leaf.

7. Roll two tiny red balls and place them on top of the holly leaves.

8. Bake in a preheated oven according to package directions for 30 minutes.

Add the beak.

1. Roll a teardrop of clay to form the head and body.

Roll a teardrop for the body and two smaller balls for the wings.

2. For the wings, roll out two balls of the same color and flatten them slightly, pointing one end of each so they are small flattened teardrops.

Simulate feathers.

3. Place the wings on a work surface, slightly apart and with the pointed tips on the outside. Press a carving blade (notched) or small strip of cardstock bent in a V shape into the wing sections to simulate feathers.

Form a slight scallop in the wings.

4. Place the body on the wings so the wings stick out, but are attached to the body. Press lightly in place. Use a toothpick to press up in two places along the bottom of the wing sections, forming a slight scallop.

Add the legs.

5. Roll out a thin black snake for the legs. Cut this in two sections. Roll one end of each leg to slightly point it. Bend them in the middle and press the top (unpointed) section of each leg on the bottom of the body.

6. For the beak, roll a small ball of yellow (on a yellow bird, use black). Flatten it somewhat and point both ends, much as you did for the holly leaf. Bend it slightly in half and use your fingertip to press it in place, being careful not to break the beak in half.

7. Roll tiny black balls for eyes and place them on the face.

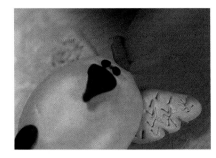

Add the crest.

8. Add a small flattened piece of red to the top of the head for a crest, if desired, or add the holly and berries as for the pig.

9. Bake in a preheated oven according to package directions for 30 minutes.

You can make birds in any color. White birds are lovely, and if you put a bit of black on the face section, you have a swan! Red and green birds together make a great holiday flock as well – try one on each holiday napkin ring. Bluebirds make cheerful decorations for a Happy "Bird" day party.

To use any of these critters as ornaments, add a loop of gold string to the back and hold it in place with a flattened clay ball the same color as the critter. Or cut a small star and press it over the string ends. Bake as directed on the clay package.

Christmas:
Egg Ornament Hanger

Polymer covered eggs make unique and beautiful Christmas tree ornaments. Refer to the directions on pages 60-63 to make the covered eggs and change the color schemes to more Christmasy colors. Use many different kinds of canes together for a fabulous patchwork effect.

You will need

long needle
18" sewing thread
18" length of ribbon, 1/4" wide
tassel

Making the hanger

1. Thread the long needle and run it down from the top of the egg and out through the bottom. Run the needle back up the way you came, leaving a thread loop sticking out of the bottom of the egg, and two thread ends sticking out of the top.

2. Put the ribbon through the thread loop at the bottom of the egg, pulling it through halfway.

3. Take hold of the needle and both threads now coming out the top of the egg and pull gently but hard enough to bring the thread loop carrying the ribbon up through the egg. Pull through until there is a 4" or 5" loop of ribbon at the top of the egg and two ends of ribbon sticking out the bottom of the egg. Remove the needle and thread.

4. Make a knot in the base of the ribbon loop at the top of the egg by bringing the loop around to form a circle by crossing itself. Put the loop top through the circle and pull carefully to form the knot at the top of the egg. Hold on to the ends of the ribbon at the bottom of the egg so they don't get lost inside the egg.

5. Tie the ends of the ribbon at the bottom of the egg to form a knot or a bow, to keep it from being pulled completely out of the egg.

6. Sew the tassel to the ribbon bow at the bottom of the egg.

Valentine's Day:
Queen of Hearts Collage

A vision in red, ivory, and gold (or any other combination you fancy), this collage piece can be framed for a whimsical wall hanging. Used as a centerpiece to an extravagantly beaded confection, or as an embellishment on a treasure box, a face always commands attention. The molded faces on page 47 can be used for this project, or use pulls from commercially available molds. Dressed up as shown here, they are suitable for Valentines – but they can be done in any number of colors and styles.

6" x 8"

You will need

baked polymer face (see page 47 for
   making instructions)
2 oz. white or ivory (mixed) clay
1 oz. red clay
Aztec Gold PearlEx powder
rubber stamps (I used Helene's Note
   #J31042 and Floral Heart #108545
   from Uptown Design Co.)
2 pieces of 8-1/2" x 11" cardstock,
   one cut in quarters
Flecto Varathane
medium stain (recipe on page 25)
decorative-edge scissors
small heart-shaped cutters if desired
1200-grit wet/dry sandpaper
gold inkpad
baby comb or animal (flea) comb
old playing cards and decorative paper
artificial flowers
white glue

Making the pieces

Making the background

1. Roll white or ivory clay
through a pasta roller at the #4 setting or by hand to a thickness of
1/20". Roll a piece as wide as the
opening of the machine allows – you
need a rectangle about the size of the
cardstock quarters.

Cut a rectangle of clay with
decorative-edge scissors, then rubber
stamp the design into the clay.

2. With a ponce bag or brush,
lightly powder the decorative-edge
scissors and trim the clay rectangle to
fit in the cardstock area. Place the clay
on the cardstock and lightly powder

the Helene's Note rubber stamp.
Press the stamp into the clay several
times, covering the entire surface.

3. Gently peel the cardstock
away, and roll the clay piece back
through the pasta roller at the #3 setting in one direction and the #4 setting in the other direction, or roll by
hand with a brayer. This compresses
the rubber stamp impressions
slightly, but they will still be visible.

4. Place the clay back on the
cardstock to keep it flat. Place the
clay and cardstock into a baking pan
and set aside for baking later.

Making the hearts

1. Roll red clay through a pasta
roller at the #5 setting or by hand to
a thickness of 1/20".

2. Place the clay sheet on a rectangle of cardstock and load the
Floral Heart stamp with gold ink.
Apply ink to the red clay and allow
the ink to air dry for a few minutes.
Until the clay is baked, the ink will
smudge, so handle it carefully.

3. Use the decorative-edge scissors or a blade to cut the heart shape
out of the clay, cutting 1/4" outside
the stamped area so a little red shows
around the outside edge.

4. Apply gold powder to the edge
if desired.

5. Press the edges of the clay on
the teeth of the comb to get a fine
lined edging, or use the tip of a knife
to score lines all around.

6. Slice this heart in half from top
to bottom. Place it in a baking pan to
bake later.

7. Use small heart cutters or
Kemper tools to cut shapes from the
extra red clay. Stamp these with gold
ink and place them in a pan for later
baking.

8. Roll out the remaining ivory or
white clay in the same way as the red.

Stamp as before to make one heart.
Allow the ink to dry, then fold it
down accordion style with two pleats.
Be careful of the wet ink. (Remember
to clean your stamps after use.)

9. Clean all the edges of the clay
pieces by rubbing them with your
fingertip. Add gold powder to the
edges if desired.

10. Bake all these pieces for 30
minutes as directed on the package.

11. When cooled, stain the
white/ivory background piece (I
used medium stain). Scrub the stain
into the stamped areas with a plastic
craft brush, then wipe off the surface
with a rag.

12. Apply a coat of varathane to
the stamped heart pieces to protect
the ink.

13. When dry, lightly sand only
the background piece with 1200-grit
sandpaper to remove any paint from
the surface, leaving it only in the impressions.

Dressing the face

1. Use the uncut cardstock as
your collage backing. Glue decorative paper to this as desired. Place
playing cards or other decorative papers on top of this, but don't glue
them in place yet – you may want to
rearrange them later.

2. Place the white/ivory background sheet in the center of the collage.

3. Place the baked face on top of
this. Make the headdress by placing
the cut red heart sections on either
side of the face and the white/ivory
heart above the face.

4. When you are pleased with the
arrangement, glue all the pieces. Add
artificial flowers and other small embellishments such as the little heart
cutouts, beads, feathers, etc.

Wall hangings or decorative embellishments can be put together collage style, starting with decorative
papers and adding layers of clay
pieces, cloth, beads, feathers – whatever you desire. These pieces can be
scanned as computer files and used to
make wonderful cards (see page 51).

Valentines Day:
Heart Pins

These elegant hearts are so simple to make, you'll want to give some to everyone you love! You can make them into jewelry by gluing on pin or earring backs after baking, or use white glue to add them to gorgeous handmade Valentine's cards. Try them as buttons or as magnets, or as a centerpiece for seed bead embellishment.

The hearts are made by rolling clay sheets using a pasta roller or with a brayer, and impressing rubber stamps or other texture elements like real lace, textured vinyl placemats, vintage jewelry, or even the design on the ends of silverware. You can use a wide range of reds, hot pinks, oranges, and purples for some wild hearts, or muted and dusty versions along with ivory for an antique look. Pastel or pearlized effects can be very dainty!

Approximate Size:

1-1/2"

You will need

clay in Valentine colors
PearlEx powders, Fimo
    Bronzepulvers, or embossing
    powders
small glass beads or Beedz
Flecto Varathane
heart-shaped cutters or Shapelets
rubber stamps, other texture items,
    or Shadex sheets
Super Glue
jewelry findings or magnets as desired

Making the hearts

1. Condition the clay thoroughly. Mix colors if desired. Try adding a little black to reds or pinks to mute the color. This is a good way to mix colors like rosewood or desert pink. Adding a little white to red will keep it bright, as red is a color that often darkens with baking.

2. Roll the clay through a pasta roller at the #4 setting or by hand to a thickness of 1/20". You can make sheets at a thinner setting to use in collages or on cards, but for wearables, it's best to use a #3 or #4 setting.

Press the clay into a texture source.

3. Lightly powder a texture source such as a matrix tray, rubber stamp, texture sheet, or lace. Press the sheet into the texture source.

Cut a heart shape.

4. Cut a heart shape out of the impressed clay. Gently smooth any rough edges with your fingertip.

Add powder to the raised areas.

5. Highlight the raised areas of the designs on the raw clay with PearlEx powders or Fimo Bronzepulvers. Use your fingertip to apply powder to the outside edges of the pieces to rim them completely if desired. Don't get powder on areas you wish to glue, such as the backs of buttons, pins, or earrings.

6. For alternative effects, don't powder the raised areas. Instead, mix powders or acrylic paints with varathane to make a stain or faux-enamel that can be painted onto a baked and cooled piece, then quickly wiped off the raised areas to leave the color or metallic in the recessed areas.

Pour Beedz on the heart.

You can also use varathane as a glue by wiping it off the raised sections, leaving it in the recessed areas, then pouring Beedz or glitter into the recessed areas. Wipe any stray bits from the raised areas and allow to dry.

Lightly stamp metallic ink on raw clay.

7. You can also use metallic ink made for rubber stamps, and stamp designs on the clay with less pressure for a smooth surface effect. This can be done on raw or baked clay, but I prefer the results on raw clay.

8. Bake the clay according to package directions for 30 minutes.

9. After baking, seal with varathane. This is particularly important if you used powders, paints, or metallic leaf.

10. Use Super Glue to attach jewelry findings to the back.

WINTER GALLERY

Sarajane Helm. "Winter Mask."

Tamila Darling. Snowflake bracelet.

Sarajane Helm. "Santa and Mrs. Claus with a Sack Full of Toys."

Sarajane Helm. Necklace and earrings.

Robin Williams. "Santa Ornament."

Dawn Naylor. "Mom...I GOTTA go!"

Sarajane Helm. Ornaments and beaded garlands.

Judy Belcher. "Lights of Christmas" bracelet.

Sarajane Helm. Wear a Christmas necklace—or drape it on the tree!

Tamila Darling. "Candy 'n' Cookies."

Photo by SnapShots.

Photo by SnapShots.

Leigh Ross. "Millenium Garden" beads.
Beads make wonderfully dainty ornaments
on a small tree!

Sarajane Helm. "Madam's
Happy New Year" and detail.
The champagne bottle and
glasses are one foot to two
inch scale.

Dinko Tilov. "Birds and Christmas Elf."

Dinko Tilov. "Tree and Ax."

Dinko Tilov. "Purple Genie With
Christmas Hat."

Sarajane Helm. "Carolers," 5" tall.

Photo by Hema Hibbert.

Hema Hibbert. "Angel Collection."

Photo by Don Sweeney.

Linda Hess. "Nativity Chess Set."

Dotty McMillan. "Angel."

Photo by David Koontz.

Tamila Darling. "Tangled."

Photo by SnapShots.

Tamila Darling. "Gingerbread Baker."

Ellen Berne. "Celebrations of Kwanzaa" mask pins.

Photo by Barbara Hunt.

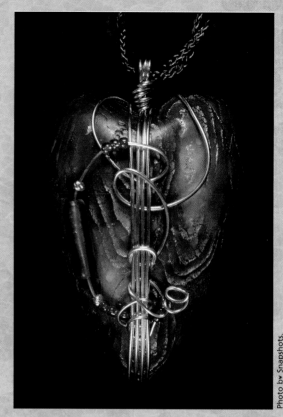

Photo by Snapshots.

Kathy Weaver. "Mokume Gane and Wire Wrap Heart."

Ellen Berne. "St. Valentines Day Clock, Necklace, and Pen Set."

Photo by Barbara Hunt.

Sarajane Helm. Filigree egg ornaments.

Photo by Tim Thayer.

Kathleen Bolan. "Ms. Fortunes," polymer clay, PMC, and wire.

Susan Bradshaw. "Chinese New Year Dragon."

BIBLIOGRAPHY

Create a Polymer Clay Impression. Sarajane Helm, Krause Publications, Iola, WI, 2001.

Creative Clay Jewelry. Leslie Dierks, Lark Books, Ashville, NC, 1994.

Traditional Stencil Designs From India. Pradumna and Rosalba Tana, Dover Publications, Inc., New York, NY, 1986 (Dover Pictorial Archive Series).

Masks Around The World and How to Make Them. Shaaron Cosner, David McKay Co., Inc., New York, NY, 1979.

Tribal Arts-Africa, Oceania, Southeast Asia. Berenice Geoffroy-Schneiter, The Vendome Press, New York, NY, 2000.

American Holidays and Special Days. George Schaun, Maryland Historical Press, Lanham, MD 1986.

Curious Customs. Tad Tuleja, The Stonesong Press, Inc., New York, NY, 1987.

Celebrations Around the World. Carole S. Angell, Fulcrum Publishing, Golden, CO, 1996.

The Big Book of Fabulous Fun Filled Celebrations and Holiday Gifts. Jim Fobel and Jim Boleach, Gladstone Books Inc., New York, NY, 1978.

Eggs Beautiful. Johanna Luciow, Harrison, Smith-Lund Press, Minneapolis, MN, 1975.

Japanese Design Motifs – 4260 Illustrations of Japanese Crests. Dover Publications, Inc., New York, NY, 1972 (Dover Pictorial Archive Series).

Celtic Art–The Methods of Construction. George Bain, Dover Publications, Inc., New York NY, 1973.

Designs and Patterns From Historic Ornaments. W. and G. Audsley, Dover Publications, Inc., New York, NY, 1968 (Dover Pictorial Archive Series).

Make Doll Shoes Vol. I, II. Lyn Alexander, Hobby House Press, Inc., Grantsville, MD, 1989.

Snow Crystals. W.A. Bentley and W.J. Humphreys, Dover Publications, Inc., New York, NY, 1962.

The Visual Dictionary of Plants. Eyewitness Visual Dictionaries, Dorling Kindersley, Inc., New York, NY, 1992.

Primitive Art-PreColumbian/North American Indian/African/Oceanic. F. Anton, F. Dockstader, M. Trowell, H. Nevermann, Harry N. Abrams Inc., New York, NY 1979.

Butterflies of the World. H.L. Lewis, Harrison House, New York, NY 1987.

ARTIST CONTACT INFORMATION

BrendaLea Abbott
720 W. Park St.
DuQuoin, IL 62832-1144
618-542-4572
prpldy@accessus.net
http://www.angelfire.com/il/blea

Lashonne Abel
130 Inverness Plaza #241
Birmingham, AL 35242
205-960-7003
themrp@bellsouth.net
Lashonne Abel Designs

Deborah and Marah Anderson
265 N. 13th St.
San Jose, CA 95112
408-998-5303
Maraha@aol.com
http://www.geocities.com/
thousand_canes
A Thousand Canes

Sherry Bailey
5 Custer Circle
Nashua, NH 03062
603-595-8225
sherry@bybailey.com

Joanne Banuelos
3238 Fallen Oak Ct.
San Jose, CA 95148
408-274-5368
rojovanban@aol.com

Sandra Beach
507 1st Ave. NE
Hillsboro, ND 58045
701-636-5063
sbea@rrv.net

Judy Belcher
414 Forest Brook Dr.
St. Albans, WV 25177
304-727-3943
JSBEL@msn.com
St. Nick Nacks

Colleen "Sunni" Bergeron
sunnisan@sunnisan.com
http://sunnisan.com/crafts/
polyclay.html

Ellen Berne
5 VanDyck Ct.
Potomac, MD 20854
301-385-5712
elelbe@erols.com

Kathleen Bolan
1606 Vernon
Trenton, MI 48183
734-675-3099
kbolan@borntobead.com
Born To Bead

Susan Bradshaw
PO Box 413
Moss Landing, CA 95039
831-768-8997
susan@woventime.com
www.woventime.com
Woven Time

Lani Chun
1333 Hoolaulea St.
Pearl City, HI 96782
808-386-9010
lani@ohanaexpressions.com
www.ohanaexpressions.com
Ohana Expressions

Lisa Clarke/Polka Dot Creat.
PO Box 172
Stirling, NJ 07980
908-626-1531
lisa@polkadotcreations.com
www.polkadotcreations.com

Jean Cohen
6104 Eastcliff Dr.
Baltimore, MD 21209
401-367-0488
gilcohen@erols.com

Tamila Darling
111 West Boalt St.
Sandusky, OH 44870
419-626-6885
tamila@simplydarling.com
http://simplydarling.com
Simply Darling Creations, Inc.

Dawn Lee Dykes
dykes_g@bellsouth.net
Dawn's Designs

Bill GirarD/GirarD Studios
1628 Sagebrush Trail SE
Albuquerque, NM 87123
505-298-1629
bill@billgirard.com
http://www.billgirard.com

Becky Green
204 Mill Lake Rd.
Battle Creek, MI 49017
269-721-3598
bbg@mei.net

Lori Greenberg
34522 N. Scottsdale Rd.
#D8453
Scottsdale, AZ 85262
602-570-2000
info@abundancebox.com
Abundance Box

Barbara Hart
Columbus, OH
serendipity@insight.rr.com
Chameleon Clay

Ian Helm
PO Box 263
Hygiene, CO 80533-0263
303-684-9069
ichelm@aol.com

Sarajane Helm
PO Box 263
Hygiene, CO 80533-0263
303-684-9069
sarajane@polyclay.com
www.polyclay.com
Sarajane's

Linda Hess
24 Sydney Lane
Stafford, VA 22554
540-288-0016
polymcrcrcations@aol.com
…By Linda

Janis Holler
5821 WCR 8E
Berthoud, CO 80513
970-532-3982
kkummli@compuserve.com
Loco Lobo Designs

Janet Hoy
j.k.hoy@worldnet.att.net

Helen Hughes
Helensclayart@attbi.com

Judy Jaussaud
738 College St.
Milton-Freewater, OR 97862
jaussaud@bmi.net
Items of Elegance and
Wearable Art by Judy
Jaussaud

Denita Johnson
djoneofakind@aol.com
http://www.djoneofakind
crafts.com
DJ's One Of A Kind

Donna Kato
PO Box 209
Florissant, CO 80816
719-748-5114
dkato@pcisys.net
http://www.prairiecraft.com
Prairie Craft

Hazel Keyes
RR 1, Box 264
Kingsley, PA 18826-9758
570-756-3334
catbyte1@yahoo.com
www.bearwithmedesigns.com
Bear With Me Designs

Ellen Knauer
511 Norway Ave.
Silverton, OR 97381
503-873-2811
eeknauer@aol.com

Z Kripke
8437 Sugarman Dr.
La Jolla, CA 92037-2226
858-453-6427
zdkripke@san.rr.com
http://artistathome.com/
zdkripke/
Just Claying Around

Julie Leir-Van Sickle
Julie@DancinJules.com
DancinJules.com

Tonja Lenderman
PO Box 704
Chewelah, WA 99109-0704
509-935-8207
tkaylcn@yahoo.com
http://home.ceturytel.net/
tkaylen/index.html

Jane Mahneke
5528 Tellina Way
Santa Barbara, CA 93111-1444
805-967-5481
jmahneke@housing.ucsb.edu

Rose Mary Martin
Rmmccm@aol.com

Layl McDill
2723 Taylor St. NE
Minneapolis, MN 55418
612-781-6409
claysquared@aol.com
www.claysquared.com
Clay Squared To Infinity

Dotty McMillan
7060 Fireside Dr.
Riverside, CA 92506
714-532-5032
dmcmillan01@earthlink.net
www.kaleidoscopes4u.com
Simply Ridiculous Designs

Bonnie Merchant
19634 S. Ferguson Rd.
Oregon City, OR 97045
503-632-7012
bonita@fabulousstuff.com
www.fabulousstuff.com
Fabulous Stuff

Dawn Naylor
3 Ureco Terrace
Worcester, MA 01602
586-798-0796
dzyns@usa.com
http://wwmywebpage.
netscpae.com/dn543
D-zyns

LynnDel Newbold
ldelli@excite.com

Karen Omodt
133 Ridgecrest Rd.
Georgetown, TX 78628
512-869-1902
kaomodt@cox-internet.com

Nancy Osbahr
1215 Belleview Dr.
Ft. Collins, CO 80526
970-377-3253
ckhearts@frii.com
Checkered Heart Studio

Olga Porteous
1012 Edgemont Place
San Diego, CA 92102-2336
619-234-8100
olgasart@yahoo.com
Olga Porteous Designs

Ann Raymond
PO Box 100
Sunset Beach, CA 90742
annarte@msn.com

Ronnie
ronica447@hotmail.com

Leigh Ross
610 5th Ave.
Bradley Beach, NJ 07720
732-776-6576
sincereleigh@PoBox.com
www.polymerclaycentral.com
Polymer Clay Central

Chris Salek
PO Box 595
Hinsdale, MA 01235
413-655-2562
fairtradevt@myexcel.com

Jen Santoro
Rochester, NY
jensantoro@earthlink.net
superluckywish.com

Janet Scheetz
422 N. Huntington Ave.
Margate, NJ 08402
609-823-5799
whimsicology@aol.com
Whimsicology

Sylvia Schmahmann
Encinitas, CA
760-635-1550
sylviaschmah@yahoo.com
New World Creations

Cecelia Shepherd
cecelia@cybernightdesign.com
cybernightdesign.com

Carol L. Simmons
4900 East Ridge Dr. S
Fort Collins, CO 80526
970-229-0370
csim@frii.com

Judith Skinner
PO Box 12251
Prescott, AZ 86304
judith@artsmountain.com
www.artsmountain.com
JASI

Denise Standifer
deniseinaustin@excite.com
http://tanstaafl512.tripod.com

Melody Steeples
inspiredobjects@yahoo.com

Dinko Tilov
610 5th Ave.
Bradley Beach, NJ 07720
dinkos@yahoo.com
http://www.dinko
Dinko's Critters out of Daystar
Workshop

Jan VanDonkelaar
Bellbrook, OH
clay4me@who.rr.com

**Stefanie Wagner and
Mary Lu Elliot**
9378 Bennoel Way
Elk Grove, CA 95758
claydaze@citilink.net
www.claydaze.com
Claydaze

Kathy Weaver
318 Camp St.
Sandusky, OH 44870
clay57@aol.com
www.artistictreasures.us
Artistic Treasures

Robin Williams
444 W. Main St.
Adrian, MO 64720
816-297-8777
robwillsee@aol.com
http://hometown.aol.com/
robwillsee/robinfimo.html

Pam and Heather Wynn
PO Box 6474
Gulf Breeze, FL 32563-6474
850-916-1133
wynnfour@aol.com